Ex Libris

WAR AIMS AND STRATEGIC POLICY IN THE GREAT WAR 1914-1918

WAR AIMS AND STATEGIC POLICY IN THE GREAT WAR 1914-1918

Edited by

BARRY HUNT and ADRIAN PRESTON

CROOM HELM LONDON

ROWMAN AND LITTLEFIELD TOTOWA N.J.

© 1977 Barry Hunt and Adrian Preston
Croom Helm Ltd, 2-10 St John's Road, London SW11

British Library Cataloguing in Publication Data

War aims and strategic policy in the Great War,
    1914-1918.
    1. European War, 1914-1918 2. Strategy –
    History
    I. Hunt, Barry II. Preston, Adrian
    940.4'01   D511

    ISBN 0-85664-597-4

First Published in the United States 1977 by
Rowman and Littlefield
81 Adams Drive
TOTOWA, New Jersey.

Library of Congress Cataloging in Publication Data

Military History Symposium (Canada), 3d, Royal Military
    College, 1976.
    War aims and strategic policy in the Great War, 1914–1918.

    Includes bibliographical references and index.
    1. European War, 1914–1918–Causes–Congresses.
2. Strategy– Congresses. I. Hunt, Barry. II. Preston,
Adrain W. III. Title.
D511.M535 1977   940.4'01   77-23577
ISBN 0-87471-872-4

Printed in Great Britain
by Redwood Burn Ltd, Trowbridge and Esher

CONTENTS

Preface

PREFACE

The bulk of the papers comprising this book were originally presented in a slightly different form to the Third Annual Military History Symposium held at the Royal Military College of Canada on 25 and 26 March, 1976. The theme of this Symposium, like that of its predecessors, was not a strictly or technically military one, but dealt with 'War Aims and Strategic Policy During the Great War, 1914-1918'. This book is an attempt to preserve its proceedings and to generate a more wide-ranging discussion than was possible within the close confines of the Symposium. Without the generous financial and administrative support of DND and the Canada Council, this Symposium could not have been held at all and to them we are most grateful. We are especially indebted to the Commandant, Brigadier-General W.W. Turner, who first inspired these symposia and who has always placed freely at our disposal his time and advice. Once again, our secretary, Mrs Karen Brown, has been a model of efficiency in preparing this book for the press. Finally, we wish to thank our publisher, David Croom, who managed to attend the Symposium to hear the papers at first hand.

B.D. Hunt
A.W. Preston

INTRODUCTION

Barry D. Hunt

> The fact is that the first war of the century illustrates the transition toward the absolute form of war whose political stake the belligerents are incapable of specifying.
>
> Raymond Aron, *War and Peace*

> The pertinence of the rule of reason is readily accepted for much lesser issues, but where war is concerned we are usually guided by faith, tradition, and passion. It is inescapable, however, that unless it is in pursuit of a reasonable political objective, any nation resorting to war is simply perpetuating wanton destruction of life and goods on a vast scale. The appearance of order imposed on the process by the use of military organisation and method only makes the destruction greater and more efficient.
>
> Bernard Brodie, *War and Politics*

Even a perspective of six decades has done little to lessen the feeling that the Great War was a senseless catastrophe, an incomprehensible tragedy which once begun seemed to set loose forces which cynical statesmen and myopic generals could barely comprehend, much less control. Propelled by a grim self-induced logic and sustained by propaganda that helped to justify the enormous costs, the war persisted until peace finally happened four years later only to reveal that the world it was fought to preserve had been utterly destroyed in the process. It remains the prime example of the price to be paid for ignoring that commonplace, yet vital, notion of Clausewitzian theory that the questions of why and for what political purposes wars are fought must govern all considerations of means or military strategy. Subsuming all of Clausewitz's writings was the warning that wars shaped solely by the imperatives of military possibilities and free of the overriding controls of political reason could very quickly take on the characteristics of a hideous cancer whose unpredictable rampages the victims can only watch and endure. In our own generation, the implications of nuclear technology have given Clausewitz's teachings a compelling new poignancy and, increasingly, he has become the focus of a much wider reassessment. Yet, if it is now generally conceded that Clausewitz's

9

emphasis on the primacy of political aims was ignored in World War I, it is still difficult to explain why. Equally difficult to define is the impact of this omission on the thinking of statesmen and generals throughout the war and at its conclusion when, in the rush to peace, questions of disposing of the defeated enemy exposed for all to see the complex and often conflicting ambitions of the victors.

Recent research — including the major works of the contributors to this volume — has largely destroyed the fallacy that most of the powers declared war in 1914 without any clear perceptions of why and to what ultimate end. To be sure, their public pronouncements on war aims were often imprecise. But these ambiguities reflected not only the enormous difficulties of formulating aims, but also the practical political and diplomatic arguments against specifying them too precisely. As the essays that follow suggest, war aims were the subject of frequent if not altogether systematic examinations, though decisions to publicise the results hinged on a wide variety of considerations affecting both national and alliance politics. Many variables came into play in this complicated equation of different interests, reflexes and personalities; and not the least of these were the unsettling influences of rapidly changing conditions and opportunities. In this respect, circumstance was an especially powerful and, by its nature, unpredictable force. If strategic theory or military doctrine seemed to suggest particular options for the generals, it offered few such guideposts for their political superiors. As Lord Esher observed to Maurice Hankey in March 1915:

> Why . . . do we worry about history? Julian Corbett writes one of the best books in our language upon political and military strategy. All sorts of lessons, some of inestimable value, may be gleaned from it. No one, except perhaps Winston, who matters just now, has ever read it . . . Obviously, history is written for school-masters and armchair strategists. Statesmen and warriors pick their way through the dusk.[1]

Such an expression of frustration from one so intimately involved in British military affairs poses interesting questions as to how and where the work of theorists makes it impact in the world of practical affairs Esher's awareness that somehow events were moving along paths other than those which reason might suggest was no isolated reaction, though it is all the more noteworthy when one considers that few senior soldiers experienced similar misgivings.

   This imperviousness to doubt is all the more alarming when one
reflects on the unusual degree of control which all General Staffs were
given and the extent to which purely military assessments directly
influenced the evolution of national policies. The fact is, before the war,
the Generals were convinced that they held the answers to their nations'
needs — the most obvious of these was enshrined in the German
Schlieffen Plan and the French Plan XVII. Even after the opening weeks
of the war exposed the shallowness of their professional wisdom, they
persisted in their appetites for more and more offensives all the while
disdaining the hesitant politicians who, to them, seemed overly sensitive
to the rising costs in blood and treasure. Yet to attribute these ten-
dencies to sheer military incompetence or obstinancy is inaccurate and
leads nowhere. For as Professor Michael Howard suggests about the
British generals, and presumably his view could be extended to the
others as well:

> These men were not fools, and they certainly were not Blimps. The
> policies they advocated certainly led to unforeseen results; but their
> advocacy was based not on prejudice, but on hard and, within its
> limits, clear thinking, after careful examination of possible alter-
> natives. Not, it must be admitted, of *all* alternatives.[2]

Their military competence was, generally speaking, not at issue. They
were with justification regarded as a highly-trained professional élite,
products of a process of steady reform in nineteenth-century military
education, organisation and thought.
   But this same process of reform was itself an important contributing
factor to those 'limits' to 'clear thinking' as late nineteenth-century
military professionalism became increasingly exclusive in outlook. Excessive preoccupation with technical-materialist questions of means led
them to ignore, or treat as no longer relevant, Clausewitz's emphasis on
the primacy of political ends.
   This raises the question of the nature of Clausewitz's impact on his
military contemporaries and heirs. Virtually from the moment *On War*
was first published in 1832, his writings were recognised by the German
military as something exceptional. Within a very few years, as the first
translations appeared in French and Dutch in the 1840s and in English
(1873), his reputation as Prussia's most significant military theorist was
established. Why this should have been so is far from obvious, for as
Wilhelm Rustow observed in 1867, Clausewitz was 'well-known but

little read'.[3] Max Jähns, the military historian, shared the same suspicion. He acknowledged the widespread influence of Clausewitz's ideas in the German army, but also noted: 'There is something strange about Clausewitz's influence, it is almost mystical; his writings have actually been read far less widely than one might suppose . . .'[4]

These comments suggest that Clausewitz's influence stemmed not from any widespread intellectual appreciation of his examination of war as a social and political phenomenon, but rather from a more general cause; namely, his personal connections with the great Prussian military reformers Scharnhorst and Gneisenau, and the influence of his major disciples, the elder Helmuth von Moltke and von Schlieffen. The complexities of his text — in part the result of its unfinished nature, and also his methodology of subjecting his observations to the dialectical analysis of German idealistic philosophy — undoubtedly contributed to his obscurity and increased the possibilities of misinterpretations. But they also provided a kind of doctrinal gloss which helped to legitimise much that followed and was argued in his name. Professor Peter Paret has argued that in Wilhelmine Germany, Clausewitz 'became honoured as the intellectual witness of the Reform Era, the theoretician counterpart of the great charismatic leaders — the Blüchers and the Yorcks . . .'[5] Yet his approach and methodology, far from being recognised as the basis of his most original achievement, were largely written off as mere stylistic affectations of an earlier generation of German philosophers. The soldiers focused instead on the more practical, and secondary, aspects of his thinking; in particular, his concern with moral forces in war, the role of genius, offensive spirit and the place of battle — aspects which ran more closely in the direction of the mainstream of late nineteenth century military thought. In this important respect, it was the views of the elder von Moltke which predominated in Imperial Germany.

As one of Clausewitz's most intelligent disciples and, from 1857, as Chief of the Prussian General Staff for over thirty years, von Moltke played the leading role in bringing Clausewitz to the attention of his contemporaries. Yet neither in his writings nor his actions — especially his spectacular achievements in the 1866 and 1870 wars of unification and his famous clash with Bismarck over the shelling of Paris — is there to be found any fundamental acceptance of Clausewitz's insistence on the subordination of military means to political purpose.[6] Not that Moltke considered Clausewitz wrong in his views, but simply no longer relevant in the prevailing circumstances. His successors generally en-

dorsed this assessment. In 1905, von Schlieffen contributed the Introduction to the fifth German edition of *On War* in which passages dealing
with political supremacy were altered or obscured. This had been true
of every reprint since the second of 1853 and the practice was continued in all subsequent editions issued before and throughout the war.
Others, including Marx, Engels and the historian Hans Delbrück, as well
as military intellectuals like Wilhelm Rüstow and von Caemmerer,
would contest this Moltke-Schlieffen perspective, but in terms of practical effect on professional thinking, they represented a minority view.
Far more expressive of contemporary opinion were the widely-read
works of Colmer von der Goltz. In his very popular *Das Volk im Waffen*
(1883),[7] he eloquently advanced the argument that in a Europe of increasingly armed and aggressive nationalisms, Clausewitz's notions of
political supremacy, though academically interesting, were otherwise
anachronistic.[8]

Nor did the German generals enjoy a monopoly on this kind of
thinking. Similar attitudes extended to the other European powers and
even the United States. In France, Clausewitz took on new significance
after 1870 as military thinkers there sought explanations of Prussia's
success or, perhaps more accurately, as they turned to him as a more
astute interpreter of Napoleonic precedent. Clausewitz's teachings, particularly those transmitted by von der Goltz, then came to shape the
attitudes of virtually the entire pre-war generation of French officers.[9]
Through the efforts of Ardent du Picq, Lucien Cardot and Ferdinand
Foch, the Clausewitzian emphasis on morale, offensive spirit and decisive battle were seized upon, given a specifically French flavour and
formulated finally into a doctrine in which war became virtually an end
in itself. Foch, who was convinced that wars under modern conditions
must be short and violent, concluded that: 'Tactical results are the only
things that matter in war . . . No strategy can henceforth prevail over
that which aims at ensuring tactical results, victory by fighting.'[10]
Through Foch and some of his more enthusiastic disciples, the harnes-
sing of these over-simplified neo-Clausewitzian concepts to a contemporary fixation on the mystique of the *furia francese* produced an
approach to war in which the problem of relating national war aims to
military strategy was completely lost to an exaggerated faith in the
notion of the *offensive à outrance*. The ultimate consequence was the
notorious Plan XVII adopted in 1913, whose central and horri-
fyingly simplistic assumption was: 'Whatever the circumstances, it is
the . . . intention to advance with all forces to the attack.'[11]

Great Britain's unique political-strategic circumstances, complicated by persistent debate and indecision about the ultimate roles of her army and navy, as well as the deeply rooted anti-intellectual biases of her military professionals, served to limit Clausewitz's full impact there. Still his works were not entirely ignored in the decade before the war. In 1909, Colonel J.J. Graham's 1873 translation of *On War*, with an Introduction by Colonel F.N. Maude, was re-issued. A new, abridged version by T.M. Maguire was also published that year. Both perpetuated the distortions of the German second edition — a situation not corrected until A.W. Bodes' translation of 1935. Clausewitz's writings were also emphasised at the army's Staff College at Camberley where, under the imaginative and enthusiastic leadership of one of the College's most remarkable Commandants — Brigadier-General (later Field Marshal Sir) Henry Wilson — the foundations of a British 'School of Thought' were laid.[12] It is perhaps going too far to suggest that Wilson's known Francophilia and his close friendship with and admiration for Foch ensured that it was an 'Anglo-French School of Military Thought.'[13] Nevertheless, Wilson's political and strategic views as Commandant at Camberley, and later as Director of Military Operations at the War Office, his absolute conviction of the need for Britain to support the French left flank in any war against Germany, and his tacit endorsement of French tactical doctrine, suggest that this French connection at least helped to ensure that Clausewitz's reception by British military opinion was as circumscribed and superficial as on the Continent. Ironically, it was Britain's leading naval historian Sir Julian Corbett and his disciple Admiral Sir Herbert Richmond who proved most openly receptive to Clausewitz. Both examined the relevance of his views to Britain's imperial maritime circumstances and went further to develop Clausewitz's unfinished concept of *limited war*, all the while questioning contemporary pre-occupations with technical matters and fascination with decisive battle. In the end, their efforts to educate politicians and admirals alike on the vital connections between political and military policy failed, at least prior to 1914. Like Clausewitz, they too had to face a current of professional thought which considered such views irrelevant.[14]

There was probably very little to choose between the various General Staffs in their disregard, wilful or otherwise, of Clausewitz's insistence on political supremacy. At the same time, however, it must be recognised that beyond demonstrating the principle, Clausewitz had very little to say by way of guiding statesmen in the formulation of war

aims. His own political views as expressed in *On War* and his other
essays and letters[15] were fragmented and in no way systematically developed. They did not flow from any comprehensive theory of international relations, nor did they reflect judgments on the merits of
particular governmental systems beyond his basic concern for political
realism and efficiency. For him, war was an act of choice to be decided solely on the basis of cold and objective assessments of the
state's vital interests. In all of this, he generally took rational political
leadership for granted.

This was of course an assumption that set aside entirely the complex questions of the statesman's role, the choices he can control in
practice, and the degree of objectivity possible in defining the state's
true interests. Only rarely do those interests bear direct relationships to
objective fact. More often than not, definitions of these interests and
perceptions of external conditions are determined by an amalgam of
reflexes and processes that are highly subjective. Domestic or internal
considerations also exert powerful restraints particularly when (or because) a decision for war involves the mobilisation of mass support.
However much statesmen may disclaim partisan motivation, they do
remain servants of their own political milieu. In Professor Arno Mayer's
words:

> They mean to sanctify this non-partisan posture with spurious in-
> cantations about their selfless devotion to an objective national
> interest which instantly demands the subordination of domestic
> policies to foreign policy. In reality, however, these decision makers
> and their advisers continue to be political actors with very tangible
> social, economic, political, and ideological attachments, if not
> interests. With rare exceptions these attachments are not dissolved
> or deactivated by the alleged requirements of the primacy of foreign
> policy.[16]

This suggests that the range for conscious choice, and thus the responsibility which the statesman bears for what follows, may be more limited
than we care to admit. It also reinforces Winston Churchill's conclusion
that in the months and weeks preceding August 1914, 'Events passed
very largely outside the scope of conscious choice. Governments and
individuals conformed to the rhythm of the tragedy.'[17]

Recent research has drawn attention to this interplay of rationality
and blunder, of domestic politics and external forces in the origins of

World War I. For example, Professor Volker Berghahn has argued[18]
that the driving forces behind Germany's transition to *weltpolitik* and
navalism were more related to internal political realities, the need to
muster the nation against the rising forces of social democracy, than to
any realistic assessments of the merits of Tirpitz's 'Risk Fleet' theory,
or of external factors, especially Great Britain's responses to the creation of a strong High Seas Fleet. This as well as other serious mis-
readings of the external environment indicate that while the soldiers
were becoming increasingly professional, the politicians had not undergone any comparable growth in their understanding of how to retain
their control over policy both before and throughout the war. Indeed,
the extent to which political control was abdicated to the military not
only in Germany, Austria and Russia, but also France and Britain, has
not always been fully appreciated.[19] And once given over, it was almost
impossible for the politicians to regain.

In this respect, a particularly formidable obstacle was the enormous
prestige that surrounded many of the senior officers and the strategic
policies with which their names were associated. The 'miracle of the
Marne' protected General Joffre for over two years from any effective
moves by the French government to replace him. Even Lloyd George,
who came to power in 1916 at the head of a Tory-dominated coalition
committed to infusing a new business-like approach to the war, found
his efforts to sack Admiral Jellicoe as First Sea Lord blocked or delayed by the political and personnel realities of his own Cabinet.[20]
Eventually, by December 1917, he succeeded although at the expenses
of a temporary alliance with Field Marshal Sir Douglas Haig, an even
more important target. But removing Haig demanded not only con-
summate political courage and cunning, but also an alternative. And it
was here that the real costs of the disastrous Dardanelles-Gallipoli campaign came to be reckoned. For failure there had prejudiced any serious
consideration of major strategic alternatives to the Western Front mentality. It had also exposed what many saw as the dangers of costly
'meddling' or 'interference' by amateurish civilians. Though it was un-
deniably the politicians' ultimate responsibility to replace unproductive
military leaders or strategic policies, they were powerless to act unless
they could advance acceptable alternatives. However much they
damned their generals' collective commitment to attrition and more
offensives, they felt virtually helpless to stop it.

As if by default then, rationality in the definition of war aims gave
way to a simpler but all-consuming obsession with what Raymond Aron

has called the 'dialectic of Victory and non-defeat'.[21] The fear of losing
was heightened by an awareness that eventually some accounting for
the enormous price being paid to establish or prevent Germany hegemony would be necessary. With respect to this political argument,
Professor Michael Howard notes: 'So far as I have been able to discover,
no statesman or public figure in Britain of any party after the war was
prepared to face this question so honestly as did some of their French
colleagues and answer an unequivocal yes: the price was too high.'[22]
But during the war, it was the unwillingness to face this question
squarely, even in the first few weeks when it became obvious that both
sides' opening gambits had failed, that made compromise or a negotiated end to the fighting impossible.

In a sense, war aims became strategic instruments in themselves. Subsequent delineations of war aims in terms of territorial ambitions became for all powers the visible symptoms of success, the tangible justi-
fications for the costs of the struggle. The secret treaties between the
Allies did not necessarily reflect long-term objectives. They were, instead, a means of building inter-Allied confidence, of establishing some
common denominator to their separate ambitions. The secret treaties,
Professor A.J.P. Taylor has argued, 'attempted . . . to secure the relations of the Allies between themselves; they defined solutions for the
problems which would follow the defeat of Germany, not the objects
for which Germany should be defeated.'[23] Similarly, when it came to
any thoughts of ending the war, alliance considerations of *who* would
predominate in dictating the peace, and when, overshadowed any real
concerns for what the terms might be.

Those, like Lord Lansdowne in England and Hans Delbrück in
Germany, who tried to reintroduce rationality in the balance between
political and military policies by asking in 1916-17 why peace could not
be negotiated, became victims of this obsession with victory, discredited and repudiated by their national leaders.[24] Much earlier, in September 1914 as the Battle of the Marne was still underway, von Moltke
(the younger) had been prepared to admit, in private at least, the
seriousness of the German setbacks and the implications of continuing.
Even then, however, it was easier to replace the ailing General than
admit to failure. Three years later, Sir William Robertson, the British
CIGS, would echo Moltke by admitting that he continued to back Haig's
Passchendaele offensive 'more because I see nothing better, and because
my instinct prompts me to stick to it than to [sic] any convincing
argument by which I can support it.'[25] Robertson also urged his polit-

ical superiors to look ahead to the questions of peace aims. He was afraid that armistice talks could break out at any time: 'we may be caught unprepared and find we have mobilised for Peace as we did for war — inadequately and subordinate to France.'[26] In the meantime, continuing the war demanded optimism and an uncompromising faith that 'victory' would justify everything.

Political supremacy was not finally reestablished until the end of the war. Even then, severely strained relations between Foch and Clemenceau indicated that realigning the balance of civil-military relations was no automatic process.[27] Nor did it guarantee a return of rationality. The Armistice silenced the guns on the Western Front but not those forces which, rising from ruins of the German, Austrian, Russian and Ottoman empires, survived to fuel a continuing European civil war. This is not the place to burden specific statesmen or policies for what followed from the peace-making period. Suffice it to say that in terms of preserving the links which held the European state system together, the politicians botched up the peace much as the generals had bungled the war. Considering the number and the complexity of the issues, as well as the unique circumstances under which they had to be resolved, this is not altogether surprising. As Professor Max Beloff reminds us:

> Perhaps this aspect of the matter is too easily overlooked when we look at some of what appear to be the loose ends or dead ends of some ventures . . . The wonder is not that Paris killed Wilson, but that Lloyd George, Clemenceau, and Orlando survived; not that the treaties were imperfect but that they were concluded at all.[28]

But this is only to admit that the war had set loose forces of incalculable effect; that the peace which followed victory could not of its own accord redress the balance and ensure a return to some supposed natural harmony of civilian politics and economic progress.

In the final analysis, the issues of peace and war, policy and strategy cannot be neatly compartmentalised with responsibility for each assigned to specific leadership groups. The determination of ultimate objectives is the responsibility of statesmen. In practice, however, it is the soldiers who, by the very nature of their profession, are most immediately and consistently concerned with the problems of war. 'Regardless of where ultimate authority resides', Bernard Brodie has warned, ' . . . it is a matter of great moment that only the military and their immediate retainers brood persistently during peacetime upon the

problems of war. Those who have done the thinking and controlled the
preparations will at the moment of crisis be ready to invoke the decisions they have long since made.'[29] But this 'brooding', if it is not to
result in some repetitions of World War I experience, must be con-
ditioned by educational processes which encourage the expansion of
the soldier's intellectual perspectives. The pre-1914 experience of
attempting to 'teach' strategy by means of distilling accumulated experience and theory into a few easily remembered principles led to distortions, over-simplification, and an increasingly exclusive viewpoint.
The resultant doctrinal glosses were dangerous short-cuts to that professional wisdom which could only come from the hard and prolonged
individual study of history and war in its broadest contexts. For it is
the act of study and deep reflection which conditions the individual's
mental reflexes and produces the kind of sharply honed intellect
needed to handle the challenges of new technologies and constantly
evolving circumstance. Similarly it is the statesman's responsibility not
only to understand the nature of war and the limitations of the instruments it involves, but also to develop a keener awareness of the limits
of his own powers and his freedom of choice as a political actor.

Notes

1. Viscount Oliver Esher (ed.), *Journals and Letters of Reginald Viscount Esher*, vol. III (London, 1938), p. 221. The reference is to Sir Julian Corbett's *Some Principles of Maritime Strategy* (London, 1911).
2. In John Gooch, *The Plans of War, The General Staff and British Military Strategy c. 1900-1916* (London, 1974), p. x.
3. Wilhelm Rustow, *Die Feldherrnkunst des neunzehnten Jahrhunderts* (Zurich, 1867).
4. Max Jahns, *Geschicte du Kriegswissenschaften* (Leipzeig, 1891). vol. III.
5. Peter Paret, 'Clausewitz and the Nineteenth Century', p. 30, in Michael Howard (ed.), *The Theory and Practice of War* (New York, 1967).
6. See Ebechard Kessel, *Moltke* (Stuttgart, 1957); Eugene Carrias, *La Pensée Militaire Allemande* (Paris, 1948); Rudolph von Caemmerer, *The Development of Strategical Science during the 19th Century* (London, 1905).
7. Translated as *The Nation in Arms* (London, 1913).
8. See review article by Spencer Wilkinson, 'The Character of Modern War ', in *War and Policy* (New York, 1900), pp. 176-182.
9. Dallas D. Irvine, 'The French Discovery of Clausewitz & Napoleon', *The Journal of the American Military Institute*, IV (1940).
10. Marshal Ferdinand Foch, *The Principles of War* (London, 1918), p. 8.
11. Brigadier-General J.E. Edmonds, *Military Operations in France and Belgium, 1914*, vol. 1, (London, 1922), pp. 444-9.

12.   Brian Bond, *The Victorian Army and the Staff College, 1854-1914*
      (London, 1972), pp. 245-70.
13.   Bernard Ash, *The Lost Dictator: A Biography of Field Marshal Sir Henry
      Wilson* (London, 1968). See also C.E. Callwell, *Field Marshal Sir Henry
      Wilson: His Life and Diaries* (London, 1927).
14.   See Donald M. Schurman, *The Education of a Navy: The Development of
      British Naval Strategic Thought, 1867-1914* (London, 1965); also his
      'Historians and Britain's Imperial Strategic Stance in 1914', in J.E. Flint
      and G. Williams (eds.), *Perspectives of Empire: Essays Presented to Gerald
      S. Graham* (London, 1973).
15.   Peter Paret, *Clausewitz and the State* (Oxford, 1976), pp. 327-95.
16.   Arno J. Mayer, 'Internal Causes and Purposes of War in Europe, 1870-1956:
      A Research Assignment', *Journal of Modern History*, XLI (Sept. 1969),
      p. 293.
17.   Winston S. Churchill, *The World Crisis* (New York, 1929), pp. 1-2.
18.   V.R. Berghahn, *Der Tirpitz Plan. Genesis und Verfall einer innenpolitischen
      Krisenstrategie unter Wilhelm II* (Dusseldorf, 1971); *Germany and the
      Approach of War in 1914* (London, 1973).
19.   Jere Clemens King, *Generals and Politicians* (Berkeley, 1951).
20.   A.J. Marder, *Dreadnought to Scapa Flow*, vol. IV (Oxford, 1969), pp. 199-
      207, 329-31; A. Temple Patterson, *Jellicoe: A Biography* (London, 1969),
      pp. 177-209; Captain Stephen Roskill, 'The Dismissal of Admiral Jellicoe',
      Journal of Contemporary History, I (Oct. 1966), pp. 69-93.
21.   Raymond Aron, *Peace and War* (New York, 1967), p. 31.
22.   Michael Howard, *The Continental Commitment* (London, 1972), p. 58.
23.   A.J.P. Taylor, *Politics in Wartime* (New York, 1965), p. 94.
24.   See Lord Newton, *Lord Lansdowne: A Biography* (London, 1929),
      Chapter XX, 'The Peace Letter'; and G.A. Craig, 'Delbrück: The Military
      Historian', in E. Meade Earle, *Makers of Modern Strategy* (Princeton, 1941),
      pp. 275-82.
25.   See below John Gooch, 'Soldiers, Strategy and War Aims in Britain, 1914-
      1918', p. 31.
26.   V.H. Rothwell, *British War Aims and Peace Diplomacy, 1914-1918*
      (Oxford, 1971), p. 40.
27.   J.C. King, *Foch versus Clemenceau* (Cambridge, Mass., 1960).
28.   Max Beloff, *Imperial Sunset*, vol. I, *Britain's Liberal Empire, 1897-1921*
      (London, 1969), p. 279.
29.   Bernard Brodie, *Strategy in the Missile Age* (Princeton, 1965), pp. 54-5.

SOLDIERS, STRATEGY AND WAR AIMS IN BRITAIN 1914-1918

John Gooch

The harmonisation of the aims of soldiers and civilians is a difficult task
which has beset democracies in time of peace as well as in time of war.
In the process of harmonisation the demarcation of interests becomes a
contest, with the result that disputes over objectives become disputes
over the right to determine objectives. Corporate institutions and force-
ful individuals will fight harder over the control of power than almost
anything else, including the exercise of that power. Thus it is possible to
picture the relationship between Britain's war aims and Britain's strategy
during the First World War largely in terms of the struggle by Lloyd
George to recover the direction of the war from the grasp of Haig and
Robertson, into whose hands it had fallen in December 1915 as a result
of the British disaster at the Dardanelles. Yet this description is misleading, for at the root of the differences between the civilians and
soldiers about where and how to apply military force in order to win
the war lay not just antipathy but misunderstanding and lack of communication. Neither party fully understood what the other meant by
'winning the war' — a state of affairs for which Clausewitz provided no
remedy — though the successful transition from diplomacy to war depends upon it.

A fundamental contrast seemed to exist between Britain and France
in this respect. 'The French know exactly what they want' remarked
Lord Esher, somewhat plaintively, in 1918.[1] And so far as French war
aims encompassed the recovery of territory lost to Germany in 1871
and between August and December 1914, French soldiers and French
civilians expended their blood and their treasure for clear objectives.
Britain also found herself, in a sense, seeking to recover lost territory,
after the German occupation of Belgium, and the restitution of Belgian
integrity, together with compensation, remained her most immut-
able war aim throughout the war. The price of alliance with Russia and
France was that, in effect, their claims on the territories of the Central
Powers became Britain's claims also, although the military tended to
regard this as a high diplomatic price extorted for military forces whose
value was not always commensurate with their cost.

21

In addition to physical prizes and monetary recompense the Western democracies, and perhaps most especially Great Britain, fought for a cause: the destruction of Prussian militarism. The attainment of this vague and ill-defined objective could only be brought about, it was thought, 'if the adversary . . . was totally overthrown'.[2] But though this simple and emotive phrase appeared to harmonise the aims of both soldiers and civilians, it was the product of assessments about the structure and intentions of Germany which differed in critical respects. Thus radically different strategies could be suggested to bring about what was only superficially, the same goal.

The War Office and the Foreign Office were the chief centres of rivalry over interpretations of 'Prussian militarism' and over the objectives to which war aims must aspire in order to ensure the destruction of that militarism. In the higher reaches of the army there was a remarkable degree of unanimity on the limitations imposed upon war aims by military capacity, so that it is not too fanciful to speak of a 'military party' as one of the two protagonists. The Foreign Office, although by no means always united in its attitudes, tended over-all to take a more extreme line, one dictated by its determination to dismantle Prussian militarist hegemony in Germany. Grey and Asquith shared this avowed aim, as did Lloyd George, who by reassuring doubters in January 1918 that Britain was not fighting 'a war of aggression against the German people' enabled them to infer that the Government's designs upon the German leaders were somewhat more draconian than its designs upon their followers. A 'civilian' or 'political' party might thus be said to have existed as a rival to the military party, distinguished from the military by its intentions to dismantle the political structure of Germany, and therefore to a large extent the social structure also, once the w.. was won. The fact that a politician such as Balfour, who did not always agree with Lloyd George's strategy or intentions, supported the Prime Minister in the belief that he was irreplaceable as war leader gives further credence to the notion that such a grouping existed in practice.[3]

Sir William Robertson certainly thought that such a group existed, and that it was dedicated to opposing the military. From the moment that he became Chief of the Imperial General Staff in December 1915 he regarded himself as fighting a political battle against the civilian group in the Cabinet which was opposed to the Western Front at any and all times.[4] Realising that strategic arguments alone might not carry the day in such circumstances, he initiated a considerable private correspondence with Haig in France, Milne at Salonika, and Maxwell and

Murray in Egypt in order to provide himself with up-to-date information for use in debate. And he saw too that the military represented a political party which had to be united in the face of a united opposition. 'The great asset', he wrote to Haig, 'is the army — whose value will be fixed largely by the extent to which we at the top stick together and stand firm.'[5] Robertson's plaints that 'politicians and soldiers must each keep within their respective sphere, must work close together and in sympathy the one with the other, and remember that it has never been good policy to adopt bad strategy' flowed not from some quasi-mystic belief in the power of military capacity but from a growing awareness of the limits of what force could achieve.[6] It flowed also from his reading of how to achieve the war aims that the civilians had set, if indeed they could be achieved at all.

An ambivalence in Foreign Office policy towards Germany can be detected from the moment of Grey's access to office in 1905. Even though his first two years of authority seemed to have laid down the lines of an anti-German policy, with the Anglo-French staff conversations and the Anglo-Russian entente, yet there were indications of a bed-rock of support for a policy more favourably disposed towards Germany should conditions permit or require it.[7] That policy did appear between 1912 and 1914. It was brought about partly by the influence wielded by Haldane and partly by the replacement within the Foreign Office of the hard-line anti-Germans headed by the Permanent Under Secretary Sir Arthur Nicolson by an anti-Russian faction headed by Grey's private secretary, Sir William Tyrell.[8] This change complemented Grey's own reassessment of German policy and German policy-makers. By late June 1914 he had come to believe that Britain was on good terms with Germany and *vice versa:* 'The German Government are in a peaceful mood and they are very anxious to be on good terms with England.'[9]

Once the July crisis developed, this apparent paradox had to be resolved. The answer, in Grey's mind and in others', was that two parties existed in Berlin: a 'war party' and a 'peace party', the latter including Jägow, Bethmann Hollweg and the Kaiser. Grey's policy was to avert war — at first sight a somewhat passive policy, but in fact one calculated to give the 'doves' in Berlin something to work with. The outbreak of war in August 1914 was interpreted by the Cabinet as the victory of the 'war party'.[10] It was but a short step from this conviction to one in which a military party had deliberately prepared for and planned the war — a view which Grey subsequently took.

Thus the political version of Britain's most ambitious and most fervidly proclaimed aim — the destruction of Prussian militarism — derived from assumptions about why and how Germany had started the war. Translated into military terms it dictated victories over Germany of such magnitude as to permit changing the social fabric and the political structure of Germany. This in turn would destroy the basis of Prussian hegemony over Germany and would also end the dominance of the military over German society. Nursing these convictions civilians sought throughout the war to follow strategies determined not by what was possible but by what was necessary in order to achieve their gargantuan aim.

The military, unlike the civilians, held a 'unified' view of Germany. They saw not a 'peace party' and a 'war party, but simply Germany. This meant that they had no reconciliation to effect between false hopes and harsh reality *vis-à-vis* German policy in 1914. As early as 1902 the War Office had discarded any notions of a German alliance. Sir William Robertson had pointed to Germany's colonial ambitions and to her commercial and naval rivalry with Great Britain and had concluded that 'instead of regarding Germany as a possible ally we should recognise her as our most persistent, deliberate and formidable rival'.[11] The Director-General of Mobilization and Military Intelligence, Sir William Nicholson, concurred: 'I am afraid that the unfavourable view which he takes of the attitude of Germany toward England is correct.'[12] Colonel Henry Wilson put the view more directly in the pages of his private diary: 'The Germans, who have an increasing population and no political morals, *mean expansion* and therefore aggression.'[13]

The First Moroccan crisis and the Tabah incident simply confirmed the War Office view that Germany intended to be bound by no restraints in pursuing her national interests. In 1906 the Director of Military Operations, Sir James Grierson, and his staff were convinced that German officers were intriguing against Britain in Palestine and Egypt, a conviction shared by Lord Cromer.[14] Grierson's successor and Wilson's predecessor as DMO, Sir Spencer Ewart, held a somewhat more urgently pessimistic view of Germany's policy: in the spring of 1907 he felt war between England and Germany to be 'highly probable, if not absolutely inevitable in the course of a few years. Germany, ever increasing in population but a late arrival in the field of colonization, feels that she cannot satisfy her aims and ambitions unless she can defeat us.'[15] Sir Henry Wilson (DMO 1910-14) was thus but the last,

and most effective, in a long line of British soldiers who believed im-
plicitly and explicitly in the inevitability of a German challenge. In this
respect at least, and despite the claims of his detractors,[16] Wilson came
of a good military pedigree.

Believing that Germany had long intended to fight a war against
Britain and that in this respect Germany was an homogeneous organism,
the military were not caught by surprise by the events of July 1914 to
the extent that their civilian counterparts were. Nor were they subsequently astounded by the revelation of Germany's appetite for territorial possessions. 'Germany's ambition to establish an empire stretching
across Europe and the North Sea and Baltic to the Black Sea and the
Aegean, and perhaps even to the Persian Gulf and Indian Ocean, has
been known for the last 20 years or more' declaimed Sir William
Robertson airily in December 1916 when considering German peace
proposals.[17]

The result of these assessments and perceptions was that the
soldiers' concept of defeating Germany differed in critical respects
from the civilian one. For the soldiers the fundamental strategic objective was to inflict a military defeat upon Germany of sufficient magnitude as to cure her of her relish for a role as a world power. A sharp
'lesson in arms' would also contribute to future international order by
demonstrating that wilful interruptions of peace would meet with
prompt and effective military reaction. This view of 'Prussian militarism' dictated the strategy essential to its destruction: since Germany
disrupted international relations by gambling with force, military defeat must be inflicted upon her to stop her playing fast and loose.
Germany was therefore the main objective of operations and the inflic-
tion of physical defeat upon her armed forces the goal. Hence the pre-
dominance of the Western Front in military strategy during the First
World War. Defeat of Austria and of Turkey might meet the politicians'
aims by putting such pressure upon Germany as to make her consent to
far-reaching social and political changes; it could not meet the soldiers'
aims of demonstrating to Germany by means of direct military defeat
that military gambles would not and could not work.

The very formulation of the chief British war aim was thus the
foundation for the ever-deepening rift between soldiers and civilians
over strategy in the First World War. Its vagueness and imprecision
could allow of quite different interpretations and therefore of strategies
that were fundamentally opposed. This basic disharmony also ruled out
quite sensible compromise solutions such as the suggestion made by the

Foreign Office in 1917 that Germany become a Continental Power confined to Europe and Britain an imperial power controlling the seas.[18] The General Staff argument was that Britain was a Continental Power, whether she liked it or not, whose interest in a harmonious Europe dictated the military defeat of Germany. Even Kitchener, the least 'European' of the military authorities, did not think colonies very important in the outcome of the war.[19] Lloyd George's formulation in October 1917 of 'Military victory' — which he interpreted as driving the Germans back to the Meuse — was equally a nonsense in the eyes of the army since it would not amount to a strong discouragement to Germany to try again for European hegemony in the near future.

The extent of the gap between the soldiers' concept of defeating Germany and that held by many of the civilians would doubtless have become apparent had there been any general discussion of what Britain's war aims were, but for a variety of reasons the politicians were distinctly unwilling to orchestrate such a discussion. They feared, with some justification, that the result would be less than tuneful. Esher, who complained in August 1916 that no one 'is looking ahead and preparing for the day when questions of armistice and peace become urgent', believed that Asquith's temperament was the chief barrier to such an exercise.[20] In this case temperament was buttressed by real diplomatic dangers. Any substantial delineation of war aims could only lead to discord among the Allies,whose claims ran counter to one another at certain points. It was for this reason that Asquith made no substantial declaration of Britain's war aims between November 1914 and January 1916,[21] an omission which gave the soldiers little by way of political guidance.

The Prime Minister's policy in this respect had the wholehearted support of his Foreign Secretary. Sir Edward Grey always discouraged Cabinet discussion of war aims as likely to lead only to disharmony and discord within the Government. Thus the War Committee never ever debated war aims. The only other forum in which such delicate but crucial issues might be raised was the House of Commons; here the Foreign Office proved adept at blocking any attempts by disputatious Members to ventilate the issues.[22] There was a rationale behind the views of both Asquith and Grey, which makes their reluctance to grasp the nettle understandable and prudent. Beyond the immediate dangers of discussion lay the indistinct but daunting outlines of a problem — that of making peace — best summed up by Sir Arthur Nicolson. 'It is appalling to think of the difficulties which will arise when the moment comes for the discussion of peace terms', wrote Nicolson to Buchanan. 'I cannot imagine any peace which will be more difficult. It will practically amount to a remodelling of the map of Europe.'[23]

Britain's partnership in an alliance, which was one of the forces obstructing an open discussion of war aims, should not be underestimated, for it presented difficulties which were real and which seem in some cases to have been insurmountable — though the soldiers regarded the problem in a somewhat simplistic manner. Sir John French found his Gallic allies brave but trying: 'Truly I don't want to be allied with the French more than once in a lifetime. You can't trust them'.[24] Sir William Robertson took a somewhat more jaundiced view. 'Allies are a tiresome lot', he declared roundly, no doubt in part because he found it 'very difficult to deal with people like the French'.[25] Lack of discussion and co-ordination meant that the soldiers would have no knowledge of the limitations imposed upon strategy by the requirements of alliance diplomacy. They certainly should have known, for the limitations were daunting.

By an exchange of notes on 5 September 1914 Great Britain, France and Russia had each agreed not to conclude a separate peace with the Central Powers. In order not to have to satisfy the ravenous appetites of each other, they had added a secret clause to the effect that no party would demand terms not previously concurred in by both the others. Russia had already announced, on 16 August, her intention to create an autonomous Poland ruled over by a Lieutenant of the Tsar after the war. Then in October she unilaterally signed away Rumanian Transylvania to Rumania to enveigle her into the war. This had the effect of demolishing at a stroke any prospects of a negotiated peace with Austria-Hungary since Hungarian nationalists could no longer be mobilised in the Allied cause. The subsequent creation by the Allies of the 'nationality principle' simply confirmed the impossibility of a separate peace with the Habsburg Empire.[26]

If Russia's avowed aims affected British diplomacy and strategy, so much the more did Russia's supposed objectives; this was a matter over which Grey was more than usually secretive. Grey wanted at all costs to keep Turkey out of the war, since any Russo-Turkish engagement carried with it three concomitants. It would detract from Russia's exertions against Germany; it would have an unsettling effect on Muslims throughout the British Empire; and its location on the Caucasus meant that Britain could only lose Persia — either to Turkey or to Russia.[27] To buy off Russia in this delicate region Grey offered her first a free hand to dismember Turkey and subsequently control of Constantinople and the Straits.[28] These considerations, to which few within the Foreign Office were privy, explain Grey's tacit support of the Dardanelles expedition: though strategically dubious, it offered a chance to keep Russia out of Persia and out of Europe at the same time. Robertson, who was more awake to the prospects afforded by diplomacy than some of his critics made out, suggested in February 1916 that Britain abandon her aims against Turkey in order to get Turkey to abandon Germany and leave the war. Britain's promise to Russia of Constantinople and the Straits made this apparently sound step impossible.

Robertson raised the issue of a negotiated peace both with Bulgaria and Turkey in 1917.[29] Tsarist Russia had by this time been engulfed and with it one source of opposition to a Turkish compromise, but there remained the equally daunting figure of Lloyd George whose determination to break up the Turkish Empire was by this time firmly rooted. Turkey thus provides an object lesson in the incompatibility of Britain's military and diplomatic war aims. Military defeat of Germany dictated by 1917 the need for separate peace with Turkey in order to concentrate resources, but civilian determination to break up Turkey made any such adjunct to strategy impossible. The civilian strategy was the more illogical in that the break-up of the Turkish Empire would bring in its train vast new commitments which were undesirable, as the de Bunsen Committee had recognised in 1915.[30]

If the military in Britain were unaware of the degree to which relations with their Eastern ally and diplomatic calculations about the future of Turkey were shaping war aims, and thereby shaping strategy also, they certainly had their suspicions about the well-springs of French strategy. Robertson was always opposed to the Salonika expedition, for the very good reason that it could in no way contribute to the defeat of Prussian militarism as he understood the term. He was also convinced that its purpose was anything but strategic:

The expedition was wrong from the start, and it will be wrong until the end, and it always has been and still is for purely French political purposes. Last Autumn we sent further troops there, to please the French, in a futile endeavour to assist Rumania. We were told that if we did not send them it would mean the downfall of the French Government and we have been told so every time the question has come up. If we do not mind [he added plaintively] we shall lose this war in our vain attempts to bolster up the French Government.[31]

Robertson's suspicions were also aroused by the enthusiasm with which France demonstrated her willingness to aid Sherif Hussein after he had risen in revolt in the Hedjaz in June 1916. He felt that Britain and France had a common strategic interest in defeating Germany on the Western Front, and yet peripheral operations in such a far-flung theatre as Arabia ran patently against that interest. His suspicions were never resolved, but here again French war aims acted as an embarrassment as far as the formulation of Britain's military strategy was concerned.

Suspicion about France's designs coloured the decisions of politicians as well as of soldiers, thereby adding another force to the many which shaped war aims. Sir Edward Grey accepted on 4 March 1915 a vast list of Russian demands for Turkish territory, comprising Constantinople, the Western Bosphorus, Marmora, the Dardanelles and Southern Thrace, formulated in order to outmanoeuvre the French, who appeared to be using Britain as a catspaw with which to block Russian demands without themselves having to take the blame for obstructing their Russian ally.[32] Wariness of French intentions shaped Britain's diplomacy and thereby her war aims as much as it shaped her strategy, if not more so, and fear of the ally rather than of the opponent was to lead to Robertson's attempt in the summer of 1916 to elucidate precisely what Britain's war aims comprised.

The failure to clarify or co-ordinate the war aims of soldiers and civilians, though perfectly explicable in the light of the tangled and conflicting pressures to which the aims were subject, had the unfortunate but predictable result that long-term objectives were phrased in a vague and misleading way. Esher's assertion that Britain was fighting for 'our right to live to-day as a free people' was, at least superficially, little removed from Haig's 'great issue at stake, the existence of England as a free nation'.[33] Esher also framed the overriding war aim for which soldier and politician alike strove: a peace which would give some security to the civilised world for a good many years to come'.[34] Here the 'destruction of Prussian militarism' was at its most misleading: soldiers and civilians envisaged quite different means of bringing it about by 'freeing mankind from German tyranny'. A common terminology concealed different goals and different means.

The soldiers' aim was to conduct strategy in a way which would force Germany to abandon her 'mailed fist' policy in international affairs and give trustworthy guarantees of future peace in its stead.[35] 'Our aim is, as I understand it, to deal German despotism such a blow as will for generations to come prevent a recurrence of the horrors of the last two and a half years' wrote Robertson in 1917.[36] The relationship between this aim and the Western Front strategy lay in the conviction that such an impact could only be gained by a direct defeat of Germany's armies in the west; knocking away her props was not there-fore a viable alternative strategy for it would not gain the same goal — as much a moral as a physical one. Peripheral strategies would only dissipate finite Allied resources — of whose limitations the soldiers were all too well aware — and erode the morale of the armies, whilst still not resulting in the defeat of the German army. They thus seemed round-about routes leading back to the same starting point. This reasoning was the bed-rock of military strategy and even Robertson's successor as CIGS, Sir Henry Wilson, concurred in it. 'We must beat the Boche army if we want a real peace' he confided to his diary on 1 August 1918.[37] But defeat of Germany did not extend to the widespread social and political changes envisaged by some of the civilians. Haig put the point directly to the King: 'Few of us feel that the "democratising of Ger-many" is worth the loss of a single Englishman.'[38]

If the military had a more subtle understanding of the aims of the war and of how those aims determined strategy than has often been suggested, they also had a more realistic awareness of the potentiality that the Western Front strategy offered for victory than afterwards appeared the case. Though Sir John French might claim in January 1915 in his official capacity as Commander-in-Chief of the Expeditionary Force that breakthrough was possible on the Western Front and that there were no other theatres where decisive results might be obtained, privately he held rather different views.[39] The British ambassador to France reported that the general did not contemplate 'the possibility of the Franco-British armies penetrating far into Germany nor the possi-bility of Russian troops getting to Berlin.' Ministers and others, French felt, 'Had walked too big about our intentions.' With remarkable pre-science, French contended that German military ascendancy could only be crushed with the aid of an additional Power or by internal break-down within Germany.[40] In the event, it was to take both to induce a partial collapse.

French's reconciliation of the limitations of strategy and the attain-ment of goals, based on his belief that the Allied armies could not go through another winter in the trenches, was that the conclusion of peace by negotiation at the first opportunity was essential.[41] Kitchener, by disposition something of a pessimist, offered a similar prognosis to one of Sir John French's liaison officers early in 1915: 'He gave his views on the future of the war, said we ought to make them ask for terms by August, and accept them by November; if another winter came on us, the peace would be a bad one, especially for England.'[42] French gave way to Haig as executor of British strategy — and Haig believed that German military power had to be beaten. Kitchener, temperamentally incapable of taking his civilian colleagues into his confidence, was replaced in Whitehall by Sir William Robertson.

Robertson believed that to achieve Britain's war aims it was essential to attack Germany; there was, he drily pointed out, 'no guarantee that the enemy will attack us if we sit still'.[43] He also believed, with a certain amount of justification, that it was possible in 1916 to achieve the destruction of German might by breaking through the German lines. And he was much more flexible than Haig in his approach to strategy. As he wrote to Rawlinson shortly after the Somme offensive had begun: 'Field Service Regulations will require a tremendous amount of revising when we have finished with the Boche. Principles, as we used to call them, are good and cannot be disregarded, but their application is a very difficult business, and I think that we still take these principles too literally.'[44] It was not until Nivelle's attack on the Aisne in April 1917 had failed that Robertson adopted the strategy of attrition — the breaking down of the German army by inflicting on it more losses than it could inflict upon the Allies.[45] As his robust spirit was eroded by the resistance of the Germans and the antics of Lloyd George, Robertson lost confidence in the Western Front strategy until by the autumn of 1917 he was confessing that 'I stick to it more because I see nothing better, and because my instinct prompts me to stick to it than to [sic] any convincing argument by which I can support it.'[46] Yet nine months later his rival and his successor, Sir Henry Wilson, admitted the strategic logic of Robertson's policy in pointing out to the Imperial Conference that it was necessary to get a decision both in the east *and* in the west.

Despite appearances, then, military strategy under Robertson from 1915 to 1918 was more moderate than civilian strategy since it was logically derived from a more moderate war aim. The War Office did not share the view expressed by Sir Arthur Nicolson that in order to ensure post-war tranquillity Germany must lose 'all her colonies, her fleet, and be reduced to a state of impoverishment'.[47] Their attitude to

Germany was both more enlightened and more far-sighted. As such it represented an articulated working-out of the implications of their version of the 'destruction of German Militarism' for which no clear parallel existed on the civil side.

The notion that post-war European equilibrium might depend upon a strong and not a weak Germany was first suggested by Kitchener in April 1915.[48] It remained in abeyance for some time because the executive departments of government were not to be invited to think about war aims until August of the following year.[49] Then Robertson took up the theme with vigour, impelled to attempt a general co-ordination of Britain's war aims primarily by a deep-seated suspicion of French intentions.

> We may be sure [he wrote to Lloyd George] that M. Briand will have very decided views, carefully worked out for him under his general direction by the clever people who surround him and who do not appear on the surface of political life. These views, cleverly and cunningly crystallized, will probably have been communicated to Russia, as an old ally of France, and not *to us*. In fact we may find the greater part of the Entente in agreement on matters regarding which we have not been consulted and to which we cannot agree.[50]

Whilst marked with an exaggerated degree of caution, Robertson's recognition that wars are won on the battlefield but peace is won at the conference table showed a considerable degree of wisdom and foresight.

Robertson prefaced his remarks with the significant warning that it might not be possible to continue the war until Germany was 'so reduced as to be compelled to accept whatever terms may be offered her', thereby cautioning the civilians that the restrictions upon strategy might make the achievement of grandiose aims impossible, whatever their desirability.[51] He then went on to point out that a strong Germany was an essential ingredient in the post-war European system in order to balance the power of Russia and the Slav States. One means of achieving this state of affairs was to incorporate Austria proper into Germany, thereby compensating her for losses on her northern, eastern and western borders and at the same time adding a counterweight to the militaristic Prussians in the shape of ten million Catholic Germans.

Robertson put these views to the Cabinet in a paper which ranged wide over the requirements of both peace and armistice. The principles of peace he contended to be the maintenance of the balance of power in Europe, in which connection he advanced his Austrian gambit, the maintenance of Britain's maritime supremacy, and the maintenance of a weak power in the Low Countries. In the course of his analysis he mentioned a factor governing peace terms of which politicians seem to have taken no account whatsoever: 'It cannot be too often remembered', he reminded the War Committee, 'that the conditions upon which peace is concluded will govern, or at any rate ought to govern, the size and nature of the Army subsequently required by us.'[52] The minimum conditions of an armistice he suggested as being the immediate withdrawal of enemy troops inside their pre-war frontiers, the immediate release of all prisoners of war held by the enemy and the surrender of portions of the fleet. These issues were to be hotly disputed in November 1918.

When this and other papers were examined in the War Committee early in October, a brief and desultory discussion rapidly drifted off into the current state of Russia and then to the need for a general 'taking stock' of the situation.[53] The chance for a central discussion of the issue of war aims had been let slip, and was not to reoccur. The Prime Minister's defence of the War Committee's record immediately afterwards on the grounds that it 'has done and is doing very valuable work; and is thrashing out difficult problems' rings somewhat hollow.[54]

Asquith's reluctance to lift the lid of this Pandora's box more than the merest fraction meant the Robertson's proposals never got the hearing and the debate they deserved. Had they done so the civilians might well have been in a better position to understand his strategy, and he their dilemmas. As it was he could only use the printed page to warn that strategy might not be able to secure what appeared to be civilian goals. This he attempted, somewhat ineffectively, to do. A general review of the military situation in October 1916 concluded with the warning that 'we must expect, and at once prepare for, harder and more protracted fighting and a much greater strain on our general resources than any yet experienced before we can wring from the enemy *that peace which we have said we mean to have*'.[55] More direct was the caveat given to Lloyd George upon the latter's accession to Asquith's presiding seat in Cabinet: 'We must not expect . . . the war suddenly to come to an end. It is much too big a matter for that. Germany is fighting for her life.'[56] The effect of these injunctions was undermined by Robertson's miscalculated response to the first German peace note. In an endeavour to inject new effort into the war at a time when the peace proposals might weaken Britain the CIGS demanded the eradication of German influence in the Balkans and the denial of an armistice

to Germany. This psychological gambit failed, since Robertson's cal-
culatedly bellicose utterances were mistakenly but generally taken to
represent his detached and considered opinion.[57]

In the summer of 1916, when Robertson's peace proposals were
made, the war was going relatively well for the Allies: Bulgaria was still
neutral, Rumania and Russia were both engaged in successful military
actions, the Italian armies were winning victories and the Germans had
failed at Verdun to break the Allied line — for such was assumed to be
their object. By the following spring everything had changed. To compensate for the likelihood of American entry into the war Russia,
Rumania and Italy were all tottering and it appeared likely that one or
more of them might leave the war. This was viewed by the War Office
as no bad thing: 'It will probably be found that we have suffered no
disadvantage by being freed from obligations which were contracted for
no reason of policy other than that of getting as many Allies as possible
on any terms that might be asked.'[58] The worsening of the general situation and the possible loss of any ally seemed to the War Office the
occasion to raise the prospect of making peace with one of Britain's
minor adversaries and of the Government's reconsidering 'the policy
which they have adopted since the beginning of the war, and which was
defined by the late Prime Minister as being intended to crush the military power of Germany.'[59] If that policy should be changed, they
pointed out, then it followed that the primacy of the Western Front
would also come into question. As to the direction of a new policy in
the light of changed aims, the War Office limited itself to the remark
that if the main trunk be found too thick to fell it might be necessary
to proceed merely to lopping off the branches.

This important approach apparently offered the chance to harmonise the aims and the strategies of soldiers and civilians; but in reality
Lloyd George was already heavily committed to Nivelle as an alternative source of military leadership and to the dismemberment of Turkey.
In any case the Sykes-Picot and McMahon agreements were irrevocably
at odds with one another. The General Staff were prepared to try to
negotiate with the Turks, though an essential preliminary in their
opinion was the scrapping of the Sykes-Picot agreement; but even in the
summer of 1917 no one had advanced to the fundamentals, and as the
Director of Military Intelligence pointed out 'before commencing any
negotiations . . . we must firstly determine what we want and what we
are prepared to give in order to get it.'[60] Lloyd George's flirtation with
the French and his hostility to Turkey ruled out diplomacy as an aid to

strategy.

Robertson and Haig persisted with the apparently senseless policy of attrition in the autumn of 1917, although on Robertson's part with considerable qualms. By now a negative force had come into play: rather than base their strategy on achieving the defeat of Germany, the British High Command were concerned to prevent a lessening of Allied pressure upon her, her recuperation and the subsequent defeat of Italy and exhaustion of France before American aid began to tell. In such a situation it might be difficult to prevent Germany gaining peace on her own terms.[61] Neither soldiers nor civilians would achieve their version of the destruction of Prussian militarism in such an event.

Robertson made a last and by now despairing effort to explain and relate military strategy and war aims in December 1917, by way of responding to the Lansdowne letter. Never at ease in the world of politicians, he began with a gambit calculated to annoy the Prime Minster: if the entente were unable to arrive at what they did want from the war, he suggested, at least they might make known what they did not want. He made again his justification of the Western Front strategy in terms of the fundamental war aim as he saw it: 'There is as yet no sign that the German people are prepared to renounce the policy which has brought on the present war, or that they realise that the doctrine of the "mailed fist" is contrary to all principles of morality. Until they do renounce this policy it would be folly to suppose that we can obtain trustworthy guarantees of future peace.'[62] Accordingly he emphatically rejected any suggestion of a truce as calculated to disperse the Entente forces whilst permitting the Central Powers to organise their forces for a fresh attack. As true to his fundamental aim now as he had been in 1915, Robertson concluded with a plea for the greatest possible military effort.

In little more than a month Robertson was gone, succeeded by Sir Henry Wilson, a general whom the 'frocks' trusted. Yet even Wilson believed in the necessity to beat the Germans rather than conclude a compromise peace, a view which he held throughout 1918.

The March offensive and the Allied counter-attacks absorbed all energies in coping with the day-to-day shifts in the war, so that it was not until the German tide had been stemmed in August that attention was again turned to war aims and strategy. The preferences of the Imperial War Cabinet were for the revival of Russia and a Middle Eastern campaign, leaving France and America to defeat Germany; but French pressure and the need to be in a position to influence any pros-

pective peace conference negated such a course. As late as mid-
September, however, the General Staff feared a combined push by
Germany and Turkey on India the following year. On the 29th of that
month the 'rush to peace' began with the Bulgarian armistice. Wilson at
once found himself in precisely the position of his predecessor; he
hoped desperately that the Germans would not also ask for peace 'as
one never knows what the politicians will do' and told Bonar Law that
Britain was tumbling into peace as she had tumbled into war — 'No
concerted action, no farseeing action — just haphazard.'[63]

Wilson now evinced a peculiar strain of imperialism in his strategy
which set him at odds with Lloyd George. In the first week of October
his advice was to occupy Serbia and then attack Constantinople, an
idea quite at odds with Lloyd George's desire for an attack on Austria-
Hungary and then on Germany. At the end of that week news arrived
of the Turkish approaches for an armistice. Wilson now swung round to
support the strategy of attacking Austria by way of Rumania and the
Danube, knocking her out of the war, and then moving on Germany
from the south and west.[64] Here the lack of co-ordination over war
aims that had bedevilled Robertson began to affect Wilson too: the
essential preliminary to such a strategy was a separate peace with
Turkey, to which the Foreign Office resolutely refused to assent.

Whilst Wilson was shifting his strategic ground in this manner indications were mounting that Germany might ask for terms. This raised an
issue closely related to war aims but one which was, if anything, even
less cogently thought out — the question of what armistice terms to
demand. Here disarray was both complete and apparent. Bonar Law,
Balfour, Milner and Wilson were all opposed to demanding the unconditional surrender of Germany; yet Wilson and Haig, the dominant
military figures, were at odds about what terms to insist upon as a preliminary to peace negotiations — Wilson at least being aware that they
might well become *de facto* war aims in the process. The dilemma was
essentially the one that had confronted the military at the outset of the
war: how to demonstrate by means of physical demands that the
'mailed fist' had not worked and could not work. Wilson followed
Foch's terms, believing disarmament essential: his list comprised evacu-
ation of the occupied territories, of Alsace and Lorraine and of the
Rhenish provinces, the surrender of a 40 kilometre strip on the right
bank of the Rhine and the transfer to the Allies of a large number of
guns, machine guns and trench mortars. Haig, by now disillusioned,
held that the Germans were not yet sufficiently beaten to accept any-

thing approaching unconditional surrender and that there was little point in forcing it upon them — 'Why expend more British lives — and for what?'[65] He therefore discounted the value of the west bank of the Rhine.

Milner supported Haig and so, by a strange animadversion, did Lloyd George. He had now fallen sway to the requirements of Empire and proposed to substitute harsh naval terms for harsh land terms.[66] On 3 November Austria signed the armistice, and in so doing provided the means to implement Lloyd George's and Wilson's strategy of attacking Germany from the south-west and west at the same time. The following day Foch's terms were accepted and a week later the armistice was signed.

The deep-rooted reluctance of Britain's politicians to discuss war aims at all was one of the chief reasons for the disharmony between soldiers and civilians and for the opposition of 'peripheralists' such as Lloyd George and Churchill to the Western Front strategy that was the fundamental credo of the military from 1914 to 1918. Rigorous debate was the only means to bring to light the radically different interpretations the two sides placed upon 'the destruction of German militarism', yet neither Asquith nor Lloyd George would permit it: only with the deepest reluctance did Lloyd George succumb to pressure from organised labour and make a public pronouncement on war aims on 5 January 1918. This is perhaps not surprising; any detailed discussion would have revealed that the aims of the civilians did not correspond in many respects with those of the soldiers, that allies had been enlisted with little or no thought to the conflicts between their aims and that there was small prospect that military means could produce the results desired by the more rabid spirits in the Foreign Office. Sir John French had been aware of this in 1915; Sir William Robertson had raised the issue in 1916, and had suggested diplomatic solutions in 1917. The soldiers, in a word, were aware of their own limitations. The civilians were, or seemed, aware only of their own objectives.[67]

The surprising thing is perhaps that when, after 4 November 1918, all the conditions existed for the achievement of their aims the politicians did not seek to inflict the crushing military defeat on Germany which was a necessary precondition for changing her social and political structure. War weariness, at home and at the front, undoubtedly provides part of the explanation. So does a reversion to imperial concerns which increasingly prefigured policy in the autumn of 1918.[68] Britain was a European power for the duration of the war and for no longer. But the decisive influence in propelling her towards armistice rather than victory was the danger always inherent in the extreme civilian strategy: that of 'overkill'. The process of social decay, once begun, was not susceptible to outside control. Moreover it was one which raised a new spectre more alarming even than that of the 'Prussian militarist'. Sir Henry Wilson put the point tersely when opting for armistice rather than victory: 'Our real danger now is not the Boches but Bolshevism'.[69]

Since the soldiers had failed to win the war, the diplomats now set about winning the peace. With dogged persistence they sought to achieve the destruction of the Prussian militarists who they believed had started the war and who still survived unscathed. The heavy burden of reparations was laid on Germany partly with this end in view. As the Permanent Under Secretary at the Foreign Office, Lord Hardinge, wrote: 'Our terms under these circumstances cannot be too hard and when the Allies have made up their minds as to what those terms should be they must be forced upon the Germans without discussion. The big stick is what bullies like them understand better than anything else.'[70] The result was Versailles. Perhaps the history of Europe in the 1920s and 1930s would not have been quite the same had Robertson's Germany been preferred to the Germany of Lloyd George and Clemenceau.

Notes

1. Esher to Hankey, 4 October 1918. *Journals and Letters of Reginald, Viscount Esher* (London, 1934-8), vol. IV, pp. 212-13.
2. M.E. Howard, *Studies in War and Peace* (London, 1970), p. 105.
3. Kenneth Young, *Arthur James Balfour* (London, 1963), p. 396.
4. Robertson Papers. Robertson to Haig, 13 January 1916. Liddell Hart Centre for Military Archives, King's College, London. I/22/14.
5. *Ibid.* Robertson to Haig, 8 March 1916. I/22/30.
6. *Ibid.* Robertson to Repington, 31 October 1916. I/33/73.
7. George Monger, *The End of Isolation: British Foreign Policy 1900-1907* (London, 1963),pp. 329-31.
8. Zara Steiner, *The Foreign Office and Foreign Policy 1898-1914* (Cambridge, 1969), pp. 148-52.
9. Memorandum by Bertie, 27 June 1914. F.O. 800/171.
10. M.G. Ekstein Frankl, 'Sir Edward Grey and Imperial Germany in 1914', *Journal of Contemporary History*, vol. 6. no. 3 (1971), pp. 128-9.
11. Robertson Papers. 'Possible German English Alliance with special regard to Turkey and the Persian Gulf area', 10 November 1902. I/2/4.
12. *Ibid.* Nicholson to Roberts, 11 November 1902.

13. Wilson Diary, 6 July 1903, Imperial War Museum.
14. Ewart Diary, 24 March 1906. Cromer to Grey, 17 and 22 March 1906. F.O. 800/46.
15. Ewart Diary, 11 May 1907.
16. B.H. Liddell Hart, *The British Way in Warfare* (London, 1932), p. 15.
17. 'German Peace Proposals', 14 December 1916, p. 1. Cab. 29/1/P11.
18. V.H. Rothwell, *British War Aims and Peace Diplomacy 1914-1918* (Oxford, 1971), pp. 45-8.
19. M.G. Ekstein Frankl, *The Development of British War Aims August 1914-March 1915,* PhD London, 1969, p. 274. This work and Dr Rothwell's monograph have been of the greatest assistance in the preparation of this paper.
20. Esher, *Journals and Letters,* vol. IV, p. 47 (11 August 1916).
21. Rothwell, *British War Aims,* p. 19.
22. Ekstein Frankl, *War Aims,* pp. 42, 76.
23. Nicolson to Buchanan, 7 January 1915. F.O. 800/377. Cited. *ibid.,* p. 194.
24. Sir John French to Mrs Winifred Bennett, 28 April 1915. Cited *Sunday Times,* 21 December 1975, p. 4.
25. Robertson Papers. Robertson to Haig, 25 October 1916 and 18 May 1916. I/22/84, 36.
26. 'Suggested Basis for a Territorial Settlement in Europe', 7 August 1916, p. 1. Cab. 24/2/G78.
27. Robbins errs in ascribing Grey's reluctance to see Turkey enter the war to conditions on the Western Front: K. Robbins, 'British Diplomacy and Bulgaria 1914-1915', *Slavonic and East European Review,* vol. XLIX (1971), p. 566.
28. Grey to Buchanan, 12 November 1914. F.O. 371/2080. I am indebted for the substance of this paragraph to Dr Ekstein Frankl's thesis.
29. On Bulgaria, see Rotherwell, *British War Aims,* p. 141. On Turkey, see 'Situation in Turkey', 5 November 1917. Robertson Papers, I/16/8.
30. Rothwell, *British War Aims,* p. 27.
31. Robertson Papers. Robertson to Smuts, 12 April 1917. I/33/45.
32. Ekstein Frankl, *War Aims,* pp. 249-50.
33. Esher, *Journals and Letters,* vol. IV, p. 163. R. Blake, *The Private Papers of Douglas Haig 1914-1919* (London, 1952), p. 215 (31 March 1917).
34. Esher, *Journals and Letters,* vol. IV, p. 139 (25 August 1917).
35. W.R. Robertson, *Soldiers and Statesmen 1914-1918* (London, 1926), vol. II, p. 276.
36. Quoted in Rothwell, *British War Aims,* p. 3.
37. C.E. Callwell, *Field Marshal Sir Henry Wilson: His Life and Diaries* (London, 1927), vol. I, p. 119.
38. Blake, *Haig,* p. 277 (2 January 1918).
39. French to Kitchener, 5 January 1915. Quoted in Sir P. Magnus, *Kitchener: Portrait of an Imperialist* (London, 1958), p. 311.
40. Memorandum by Bertie, 21 January 1915. F.O. 800/167.
41. Blake, *Haig,* p. 104 (28 September 1915).
42. Clive Diary, 5 January 1915. Liddell Hart Centre for Military Archives, King's College, London.
43. 'Memorandum on the Conduct of the War', 5 November 1915. Robertson, *Soldiers and Statesmen,* vol. I, p. 200.
44. Robertson Papers. Robertson to Rawlinson, 26 July 1916. I/35/100.
45. Robertson Papers. Robertson to Haig, 20 April 1917. I/23/21. *Contra* Rothwell, *British War Aims,* p. 7.

46. Robertson Papers. Robertson to Haig, 27 September 1917. I/23/54.

47. Quoted in Ekstein Frankl, *War Aims*, p. 159.

48. 'Future Relations of the Great Powers', 21 April 1915. Cab. 127/34.

49. 'Naval and Military Conditions During Peace Negotiations', 31 July 1916. Cab. 29/1/P1. See also Cab. 29/1/P2.

50. Robertson to Lloyd George, 17 August 1916. W.O. 106/1510.

51. Unheaded memorandum, 17 August 1916. W.O. 106/1510.

52. 'General Staff Memorandum submitted in accordance with the Prime Minister's Instructions', 31 August 1916. Cab. 29/1/P4. Robertson's most recent biographer dismisses these important ideas on the grounds that 'nothing came of them': V. Bonham Carter, *Soldier True: The Life and Times of Field Marshal Sir William Robertson* (London, 1963), p. 197. The memorandum may well have originated in the mind of the elusive Sir George MacDonogh: Esher, *Journals and Letters*, vol. IV, p. 54.

53. Minutes of the War Committee, 5 October 1916. Cab. 22/54.

54. Asquith to Bonar Law, 26 November 1916. Quoted in R. Blake, *The Unknown Prime Minister: The Life and Times of Andrew Bonar Law 1858-1923* (London, 1955), p. 307.

55. 'A General Review of the Situation in All Theatres of War, Together with a Comparison of the Military Resources of the Entente and of the Central Powers', October 1916, p. 7. Cab. 24/2/G85. Italics added.

56. Robertson Papers. Unheaded memorandum, 8 December 1916, p. 2. I/19/9.

57. 'Germany's Peace Proposals', 14 December 1916. Cab. 29/1/P11. See Robertson, *Soldiers and Statesmen*, vol. I, pp. 281-4.

58. 'Addendum to General Staff Memorandum of 31 August 1916', 28 March 1917. W.O. 106/1512.

59. *Ibid.*

60. MacDonogh to Robertson, 1 August 1917. W.O. 106/1514.

61. 'Note by the DMI', 17 November 1917. W.O. 106/1516.

62. 'The Present Military Situation, with Reference to the Peace Proposals by the Central Powers', 29 December 1917. W.O. 106/1517.

63. Callwell, *Wilson*, vol. I, p. 128 (30 September 1918).

64. *Ibid.*, vol. I, p. 140 (21 October 1918).

65. Blake, *Haig*, pp. 332-3 (19 October 1918). See Callwell, *Wilson*, vol. I, p. 138.

66. For naval war aims, see Rothwell, *British War Aims*, pp. 262-3.

67. Certain 'structural' checks also existed which ruled out Robertson's ideas of negotiated peace with one of the minor belligerents, most notably the Foreign Office 'rule' that the enemy must make the first diplomatic approach. Rothwell, *British War Aims*, p. 182n138.

68. Sir Henry Wilson remarked in his diary on 5 November 1918: ' . . . from the left bank of the Don to India is our interest and preserve.' Quoted in Michael Howard, *The Continental Commitment* (London, 1972). p.66.

69. Callwell, *Wilson*, vol. I, p. 148 (10 November 1918).

70. Quoted in Rothwell, *British War Aims*, p. 265.

FRENCH WAR AIMS AND THE CRISIS OF THE THIRD REPUBLIC

Douglas Johnson

The study of the 1914-18 war has been revolutionised in one of its aspects by the publication of Fritz Fischer's famous work concerning Germany's war aims. While the study of British war aims has been well made in a number of excellent works by such scholars as Dr Rothwell and Dr Calder,[1] for some time now it has been noted that there are very few studies of comparable value of French aims. Historians, wishing to study the war-time origins of the peace-making procedure, such as Professor Arno Mayer, or Professor Harold Nelson of Toronto, were hampered by the lack of French sources, and were unable to give the same full treatment to France as they were to other countries, or, as in the case of Professor Arthur Link in his biography of Woodrow Wilson, when dealing with such subjects as Wilson's 'peace letter' of December 1916, were obliged to make oblique and inadequate references to French sources.[2] In a notable article published in the Revue Historique in 1966, the late Professor Renouvin foresaw the ending of this situation, with the opening of the archives of the Quai d'Orsay,[3] and these archives, together with the recently catalogued archives of the French Army at Vincennes, the archives of the Chamber of Deputies and the Senate, the private papers of such statesmen as Poincaré, Clemenceau, Pichon, Klotz, Ribot and the Cambons, should provide a volume of material almost comparable to that available in Great Britain. But it is curious that historians have been slow to take advantage of this opportunity, and with the exception of a study of French colonial aims which has been published by Christopher Andrew and Dr Kanya Forstner,[4] it is a number of post-graduate students, both Canadian and British, who have consulted and who are working on this material. Naturally, there are immediate reasons for this. As Professor Renouvin pointed out, there are gaps in the archives. The collections of private papers are often disappointing. The habit of keeping memoranda in such archives at Vincennes, for example, with no indications of who wrote the document, or who read it, can make evaluation difficult.

Nevertheless I mention the question of war aims in particular because it seems to illuminate a curious fact about French historiography

41

in general. That is to say that whilst in other spheres, in that of
military history for example, the opening of the archives has led to the
publication of a number of outstanding works of scholarship, such as
that by Guy Pedroncini on Marshal Pétain, or by André Kaspi on the
American intervention of 1917,[5] there is a lack of studies about the
French experience of 1914 and 1918. Yet this was the supreme crisis of
the Third Republic. None of the other crises, such as that of Macmahon,
or Boulanger, or that surrounding Panama, or Dreyfus, equalled this
invasion, this disruption, this massacre. Yet the French military, political, social and economic system resisted all this pressure and strain, for
as long as the war lasted. The weak and divided Republic was resilient
and apparently united, and was eventually triumphant. The contrast to
1939-40 is striking. But why should this be? In this paper I shall try to
make some tentative suggestions as to the nature of the French war
involvement and policies.

   In the first place, I would like to stress the fact that the French
involvement in the 1914 war was of an extremely general nature. There
was nothing automatic about it, neither in terms of the alliance system
nor in terms of military arrangements. The details of the Franco-Russian
alliance did not impose upon France the obligation of declaring war on
Germany (and, of course, France did not do so). There is no evidence
to support the allegation, frequently made, that Poincaré, who with the
Prime Minister Viviani, was on a journey to St Petersburg and to
Scandinavia during the crisis, encouraged the Russians to be bellicose,
or that he considered the alliance to be anything but formal and diplomatic. Equally in strategic terms, the fact that the French plans for war,
the famous Plan XVII, had only recently been elaborated, meant that
there was if anything reason to delay military action rather than to
speed it up. It was notorious that the artillery arm was inadequate, and
criticisms had been raised on this matter in the Chamber as late as July
1914. It has sometimes been suggested that there were economic reasons why France saw her fate as being indissolubly linked with Russia,
and of course it is true that there were many Frenchmen who had extremely heavy investments in Russia. However, the work of Raymond
Poidevin has recently shown to what extent this form of economic
activity had been slowing up in the period after 1909, and how, whilst
French banks were reluctant to invest any more money in Russia,
Russian financiers were showing many signs of hostility to the French.[6]
One does not need to stress the fact that the idea of revenge for 1870,
or the idea of liberating Alsace and Lorraine, were not important fac-

tors in impelling any French Government to go to war, or to adopt
bellicose attitudes.

It is true that the French Government probably had very little choice
in August 1914, since the Germans were determined to remove the
military weight of France, in one way or another. It seems probable,
too, that some of the French leaders, Poincaré for example, believed in
the inevitability of war, sooner or later, and it is certainly true that
French diplomacy was most active, towards the end of July, trying to
ensure that the British Government would come into the war and that
considerable apprehension over the weakness of France, particularly
with regard to the navy, was felt in case the British Government decided
to remain neutral. The war was readily accepted by the Government,
and was accepted in terms of general politics and strategy. In political
terms this was an affirmation of nationalism, and it took the form of
the *union sacrée*. In strategical terms this was the belief in the offensive, an offensive which was not to be a riposte to the expected German
offensive coming through Belgium, but an offensive in Alsace and
Lorraine which had its own justification.

It can be argued that neither one of these measures was what it
appeared to be. The *union sacrée* was an admission that France was a
deeply divided society, and it was much more an agreement to cease
political activity over the few months which were necessary in order to
win the war, and was the counterpart to the Government moving from
Paris to Bordeaux, rather than a determined effort to form a new
political unity. It was true that unity was easier to proclaim in 1914
than it would have been two decades earlier, since the Dreyfus affair
had, in the long run, strengthened the Republic. The Republicans had a
clearer ideology and a sense of pride in an institution which had succeeded in righting a great injustice, and they had also recognised the
importance of the army and the need to maintain it. But political,
social and ideological problems remained, and whilst they could be
temporarily shelved in the expectation of imminent victory, when that
victory did not come then they came once more to the forefront and
the elaboration of war aims has to be seen in the light of the need to
establish some sort of effective political unity. The cult of the offensive prior to the outbreak of hostilities can also be seen as a device, its
aim being to compensate for the well-known weaknesses of the French
army, both in manpower and equipment. Because France was inferior,
then it was necessary to proclaim the virtues of the offensive and the
qualities of morale rather than concentrate on such matters as fire-

power or defensive manoeuvring. But once the initial offensives of 1914 had come to a halt then it was necessary to evolve a strategy which would not only take account of military realities but would also be politically acceptable. Thus the political and social situation, the elaboration of war aims and the conduct of diplomacy, the nature of strategy and military planning, have to be seen within this context.

One must begin by noting that for some time the French Government was careful to avoid making any but the most general declarations with regard to its intentions and hopes. It denied, as did all other governments, any responsibility for the war, and it only claimed the repossession of Alsace and Lorraine. Along with its British and Russian allies, the French Government accepted the declaration of 5 September 1914 (which was before the 'victory' of the Marne, if it was a victory), rejecting the idea of any separate peace and insisting upon Allied concentration and agreement concerning peace terms. But the main aims of French diplomacy were to secure France against the onslaught of the enemy, to reassure the Russian ally, to increase the number of forces which her allies could bring into action and to open new theatres of operation in which a military decision would be easier to achieve. It is reasonable to say that these were not the preoccupations of either Russia or Britain. These French diplomatic and strategical considerations were linked with those which were more directly political. It is clear that when the Président du Conseil spoke to the Chamber of Deputies on the re-opening of the parliamentary session in December 1914, his remarks on French war aims were carefully measured. He was looking to the left, politically, that is to say the largest group in the Chamber, as well as to the right. The French Government, he said, would not put down its arms and would not consent to any peace until it had exacted revenge for the outrage which had been inflicted upon it, had restored an independent Belgium, had restituted the lost provinces of Alsace and Lorraine to France and had destroyed Prussian militarism. For the left, the aim was to convince his listeners that France was acting in the name of justice and that there was no hope for any negotiated peace. For the right, the emphasis was on security and on making France stronger. Both could be satisfied provided that the Government was not forced into being too precise about its policies. Thus, even on the subject of Alsace and Lorraine, on which there would seem to have been general agreement on the justice of returning 'a la patrie française les provinces qui lui furent arracher par la force', the Government had to be wary, since there was the danger of those on the left insisting on the need for all populations to be consulted before there was any transfer of territory. This suggestion, which was officially put forward in February 1915 during an international socialist meeting in London, was clearly anathema to other political groups and would have been destructive of any *union sacrée*.[7] Within the secrecy of diplomatic exchanges also, the Government chose to be discreet. Thus when the Russian Government, either by the Czar speaking to Paleologue, the French ambassador in Saint Petersburg, or by Isvolski, the Russian ambassador in Paris, speaking to Delcassé, the French foreign minister, sought to encourage the French Government to accept Russian plans for expansion into the Straits by offering Russian agreement to the idea of French expansion into the German Rhineland, the French Foreign Ministry seems to have refused to respond to these overtures.[8]

But in spite of this governmental discretion, the French preoccupation with future possibilities and aspirations was greater than has sometimes been thought. There was a coming together of diplomatic, political, military and economic thinking, with a view to furthering French interests. This was also a response, in general terms, to Bethmann-Hollweg's revelations of German plans and the outcome of a long-standing realisation that Germany was a more populous and powerful state than France. Thus French diplomats, negotiating with the Italian Government so as to ensure Italy's intervention in the war, and taking part in the treaty signed in London on 26 April 1915, accepted that Italy should receive territories which at the time belonged to Austria-Hungary, Turkey and the German colonial empire. This represented French acceptance of Italian expansion, and in view of Italian ambitions on the eastern shore of the Adriatic, it represented also a French lack of enthusiasm towards Russian claims to be the protector of all the Slavs. Politically it was Maurice Barrès who gave the tone to certain ideas when he began to publish a series of articles, from February 1915, mainly in *L'Echo de Paris,* in which he examined the possibility of France acquiring the left bank of the Rhine or of autonomous states being set up there which would be separate from any unified German state. He saw the situation as similar to that of 1827, when Charles X supposedly thought that a successful attack on Algiers would permit, with Russian support, a general re-organisation of Europen frontiers, so that Russian gains in the Ottoman lands would permit French expansion on the Rhine.[9] These ideas, and others which were similar, received the support of a number of individuals (including historians such as Lavisse and Aulard) and there was some propaganda effort in the same direction. Meanwhile French politicians, such as the President of the Republic, Poincaré, together with Viviani and Briand, were considering the possibility of sending an expedition to the Balkans in order to compensate for the stalemate in France which had followed on the battle of the Marne. Although Joffre and other generals tended to dismiss these plans, they were to be subjected to further pressure in the same direction by their British allies and by the Russian Government which had become particularly anxious about the pressure on their forces in the Caucasus. It was the British proposals which were the most compelling since they not only raised the question of what France wanted to achieve in the eastern Mediterranean, but also revived Anglo-French rivalry and the traditional French suspicion of British intentions which no French Government could afford to ignore. Finally, it is clear that businessmen were also active in discussing what they could hope to achieve. Officially the *Office national du commerce extérieur,* as early as August 1914, had enquired how, with the help of the blockade, French products could replace their German competition in the international market, and it is unlikely that this enquiry envisaged an expansion of French exports for the war period alone. Almost as official was the *Comité d'études économiques et administratives relatives à l'Alsace-Lorraine,* presided over by Jules Siegfried, which met each week to discuss the economic and commercial content of an eventual peace treaty, whilst the *Conférence d'Alsace-Lorraine,* presided over by Louis Barthou, which sought to study the future regime of the annexed provinces, as from February 1915, was completely official. Around such activities, organisations and pressure-groups which were more representative of private interests, came into being. The *Commission des mines et de la metallurgie* seems to have been linked with the *Comité des Forges,* whilst the *Groupe lorrain* was very much the personal creation of Wendel who was convinced that the type of peace treaty which was imposed upon a defeated Germany would have to include carefully considered economic and commercial clauses. Otherwise the result would be for France a defeat within the next ten years.[10] Amongst the most outspoken of the groups which were pressing to take advantage of the opportunity provided by the war, and for whom economic considerations were also paramount, was the *parti colonial* which, from the start, claimed that the war would give them the chance of settling long-standing colonial claims, especially in German Africa, or would provide them with the occasion to take part in various ventures in the Middle Eastern territories of Turkey. Not dissimilar to the Barresien idea that there could be a sorting out of the European frontiers was the belief that the war might lead to a rationalisation of colonial frontiers.

But all these matters have to be seen within the complex character-istics of French politics. For one thing, when considering the strategic and military developments, one has to bear in mind the secrecy with which those responsible in the French Government surrounded their activities. It is difficult to explain exactly why it should have been so, but in the case of the British plan to strike at Turkey via the Dardan-elles, the French minister of the marine deliberately concealed from the remainder of his Government the obligations which he had entered into with his British ally. This concealment, which lasted about three weeks, might have arisen from Victor Augagneur's fundamental lack of enthus-iasm for the venture, and from the fact that it was only out of his fear of British imperialist ambitions that he felt obliged to go along with the plan (although it has been claimed that he was bowled over by Winston Churchill's eloquent advocacy for the Dardanelles campaign).[11] But it was typical of the atmosphere of intrigue and uncertainty which pre-vailed in the French Cabinet and which surrounded all discussion of the future conduct of the war and of French war aims. Delcasse had been even more secretive on the subject of Russian ambitions in the Turkish Empire and when, in March 1915, the Russian Government officially demanded the acquisition of Constantinople and a large area on either side of the Straits, the French Government was taken unawares both by this request and by the prompt British acceptance of it. The claims of the French for some share in the partition of the Turkish Empire were vague, and in the discussions which British ministers held and organised on the future of Turkey, consideration of French interests was very cursory.[12]

But the clearest example of the ways in which internal political and personal considerations influenced conduct of the war is to be found in the Salonika campaign.[13] The central figure here is General Maurice Sarrail who, because he was one of the rare officers of the French High Command whose allegiance to the Republic and to the ideals of repub-licanism was enthusiastic, became the favourite of the left-wing groups whose position was strong within the Chamber of Deputies. The re-opening of the parliamentary session and the widespread discontent with the stalemate of the military situation meant that Joffre's quasi-dictatorial position was constantly being criticised and that Sarrail was being recommended not only as a more able military leader, but also as a more reliable commander in political terms. The overthrow of the

Government and the destruction of the *union sacrée* appeared to be at stake, and it was with these considerations in mind that the idea of a Salonica campaign, commanded by General Sarrail, was revived in October 1915. Since November 1914, this idea had been put forward independently by Briand, General Franchet d'Esperey, General Galliéni, and possibly by the President of the Republic himself. This was an attempt to unite the Balkans against the enemy and to prevent the crushing of Serbia, as well as being a response to those diverse interests which were always stressing the importance of the French presence in the Mediterranean. But the hasty decision to send an exped-ition is to be explained by the need to find employment for Sarrail rather than for reasons of strategy or for pressing diplomatic needs. It was accompanied by confusion, concealment and intrigue concerning both Delcassé's position (he resigned in December 1915) and the attitude of the British Government. It obliged the French Government to per-sist in a policy which was highly criticised by military observers, which involved constant diplomatic collision with England, and which necess-itated French intervention in Greek politics, culminating in the depo-sition of the Greek king in the summer of 1917. The complexity and implications of the operation were thus out of all proportion to the political considerations which marked its inception. This was under-stood, but the understanding appeared to have little effect in France.

Economic aims were equally beset by complications. French business-men had for long been self-conscious about the slowness and modesty of French economic growth when compared to that of Germany, and they had formed such organisations as the *Fédération des industriels et des commerçants français* with a view to discovering the secrets of German success in world markets and to curing the paralysis of their own economic development. Prior to the war the *Assemblée des prési-dents des chambres de commerce de France* had been startled to learn that French industries were becoming increasingly dependent upon German production in certain vital areas, such as those of machinery, tools and metals, and in consequence they had called upon the Govern-ment to help stimulate exports and redress the balance of trade.[14] But the response to these complaints and suggestions was invariably that French businessmen would have to reorganise their methods of indus-trial production and commercial selling, and that many of the time-honoured assumptions of the French *patronat,* such as the existence of high tariff protection for the home market, were by no means advisable in the general interest of the French economy. The need to change was repeated after 1914 when the shortage of shells and other munitions brought heavy obligations to French manufacturers and when a number of producers complained that the high tariff duties charged on certain raw materials was, in fact, inimical to the French war effort. French producers, in such organisations as the *Comité des Forges,* resisted this pressure to change, and they were all the more anxious to welcome enthusiastically the possibility of expansion without the need to conduct any fundamental re-structuring of their organisation and procedures. Such a possibility seemed to be present when the Minister for Commerce, Gaston Thomson, issued a circular to all Chambers of Commerce in August 1914, calling attention to the opportunities which the war and the blockade gave to French businessmen to expand their own production and to supplant their German rivals.[15] Such a possibility also seemed to be present when an inter-Allied conference in Paris examined how German economic supremacy could be destroyed after the war by a series of tariff and trading agreements which would be unfavourable to Germany.[16] And one of the surest ways of ensuring the prosperity of French metallurgy was obviously by the recovery of Alsace-Lorraine and the consequent increase in French iron ore resources. But a number of metallurgists believed that the recovery of Alsace-Lorraine would create complications, and the effective spokesman of the *Comité des forges* explained both to the Senate's *Commision d'expansion économique* and to the Ministry of Foreign Affair's *Bureau d'études économiques,* at the end of 1915, how France's shortage of coal would be aggravated by the re-integration of the lost provinces.[17] For this reason it was suggested that the future French frontiers would be adjusted so as to incorporate the coal basin of the Saar (and in fact, revert to the 1814 frontiers). But whilst this would largely solve the coal problem, it would mean that French steel production would reach such proportions that there would be serious difficulties in finding markets. Therefore there would have to be special arrangements whereby French steel could enter Germany freely. Other difficulties were foreseen, such as how to prevent those German steel producers who would be incorporated in France once Lorraine and the Saar were restored to France from becoming prosperous without affecting the rights of property. How could Germany, as part of a treaty, be obliged to provide France with an indemnity in coal without causing the market to become 'troublée'? Monsieur Pinot emphasised too his conviction that the economic clauses in the peace treaty should not be regarded as permanent.

From this discussion there arose many commentaries. There were those who believed not only that the annexation ('ou plutôt la reprise') of the Saar was the French 'delenda Carthago', but also that France should have control over the Westphalian coalfields, and that the organisation of French steel exports would be the key to the French economy after the war. In this vein it was suggested that whatever else the significance of the battle of Verdun might have been, it was also 'la bataille des minerais de fer'.[18] Part of this controversy became the allegation that French strategical planning ought to have taken more account of the importance of these centres of steel production,[19] and, more pointedly, the allegation that there were those amongst French metallurgists who did not sincerely wish for the recovery of Alsace-Lorraine.[20] Within these discussions there was undoubtedly more than an academic confrontation. The *Comité des forges* had its enemies who had good economic reasons for dissidence. Thus Jules Niclausse, *Président du Syndicat des mécaniciens, chaudronniers et fondeurs de France*, represented those who used the steel produced in Lorraine and who wanted lower prices, whilst the Schneider-Creusot firm in central France was opposed to the Lorraine producers gaining too many advantages and Camille Cavallier of Pont-à-Mousson proposed the annexation of the whole of the left bank of the Rhine.[21]

In the meantime further aims and intentions were foisted on the French Government without there being any serious governmental discussion of what these aims and intentions should have been. The President of the Republic was able to refer to Briand's report on Franco-British talks concerning the Middle East as being given with 'une spirituelle imprécision',[22] and this description of how the imminent agreement on Syria was discussed could well be applied to other areas of the world. The French colonial interest was active and influential, able to impose its views on individuals without there being any general discussion of priorities or principles. In a similar way the General Staff, after surveying the Austrian-Hungarian Empire,[23] pushed the French Government into advocating the break-up of the Dual Monarchy and accepting the creation of possible new states in Czechoslovakia and Yugoslavia and the enlargement of Rumania and Italy. And whilst the French support for an independent Poland, which complicated her relations with Russia[24] can be seen as part of a long tradition, these policies in the Danube region were the outcome of quick solutions to immediate problems, rather than the result of careful consideration.

As has been pointed out,[25] from the summer of 1916 onwards,

there was widespread public discussion about French war aims and it
became apparent that there was considerable difference of opinion
between those who believed in the necessity for French expansion east-
wards and for the possible dismantling of Germany and those who preferred that France should adopt a more idealistic and democratic position towards future conquests. The French Government also took a
number of initiatives regarding Britain and Russia, and the significance
of these initiatives is underlined by the fact that they were discussed in
the French Cabinet. But, in spite of the fact that the first four months
of 1917 have been described as 'the high-water mark of British attempts
to formulate a full programme of war aims', there seems to have been
no particular British response to Briand's letter (he was then Minister
for Foreign Affairs as well as *Président du Conseil*) to Cambon, on 12
January 1917. The Curzon Committee which was set up in April 1917
to discuss future territorial changes seems to have been very suspicious
of France, particularly with regard to their ambitions in Greece, whilst
even on the Alsace-Lorraine problem it was urged that any settlement
should, as far as possible, correspond with the wishes of the population.[26] Negotiations with Russia were even more fruitless since, on the
eve of signing an agreement which had caused dissension amongst
French ministers, and which was later to cause controversy between
certain of them, the March revolution removed the Czar's Government.
The result of these two disappointments, combined with the failure of
the Nivelle offensive, the wave of mutinies and strikes and increasing
difficulty in maintaining the socialists and radical socialists within the
union sacrée, was that the French Government modified their war
aims and in public pronouncements went back to the position where
they insisted upon the return of Alsace-Lorraine and were deliberately
vague about all other means whereby they would strengthen France's
international position against Germany.

   The various peace moves during the course of 1917 obliged the
French Government to consider a number of peace conditions, but
these were less important than their reaction to the American entry into
the war and to the Bolshevik Revolution. Towards America, the emphasis was always placed upon Alsace-Lorraine, and whilst words such
as indemnity and compensation were used, President Wilson's attention
was always attracted to the simple question of the annexed territories.
Indeed, at times, his interest was attracted by the idea that the French
were not as concerned with the acquisition of Alsace-Lorraine as he
had been led to believe, and he complacently accepted the fact that

American war aims were very different from those of her allies.[27] With regard to the Bolshevik Revolution, the French passed rapidly from a moderate and reserved attitude, to Clemenceau's bitter condemnations. But the emphasis was always on Germany's exploitation of Bolshevik Russia, and there was little immediate attempt to defend France's considerable financial and economic interests.[28] France sought to come to a working agreement with the British Government, and to divide Russia into various spheres of influence, whilst at the same time giving support to the various nationalities on Russia's borders, especially Poland. The emphasis, even when intervention was favoured, and when the French sought to strengthen the roles of such countries as Rumania and Czechoslovakia, was upon the need to destroy any German hold over Russia, rather than upon a hostility to Bolshevism and to the Bolsheviks themselves.[29] With the coming to power of Clemenceau French policies acquired even greater flexibility since he was able, through his personal approach, to adapt his policies to circumstances. Thus, in negotiations with Lloyd George, it is said that he readily abandoned the aims of the French colonial party, without any prior consultation or any subsequent reporting back.[30]

Perhaps Clemenceau's action, and his rapid repudiation of many years of work, pressure and achievement on the part of the French colonial group, is an appropriate stopping-point. It illustrates the uncertainties of French war aims, stemming from the complexities of political life and of France's diplomatic position. It is of course true that other countries also experienced difficulty in establishing both their strategical and their diplomatic requirements. British ministers were often as reluctant as the French to spell out their intentions and someone such as Kitchener could be as secretive or as devious as any French minister.[31] But the French confusions, and British ministers and officials felt strongly that they were confusions, especially in Greece and Salonica, should be seen in three particular ways. That of the structure of government, so that an individual or a group could become particularly important. That of the need to have a great many plans going at any one time, and in this French war policies were a pointer to post-war policies, when the need to have strategic guarantees against Germany went hand in hand with reliance upon the Western Allies and the attempt to organise alliances with allies in Eastern Europe. And that of maintaining some sort of effective unity in war-time. The very ambiguities of France's intentions and aspirations helped to maintain a political unity, however, fragile, and enabled the Republic to survive its gravest crisis.

Notes

1. V.H. Rothwell, *British War Aims and Peace Diplomacy 1914-1918* (1971); Kenneth J. Calder, *Britain and the origins of the New Europe 1914-1918* (1976).
2. Arno J. Mayer, *Political origins of the New Diplomacy 1917-1918* (1959); Harold I. Nelson, *Land and Power. British and Allied Policy on Germany's Frontiers 1916-1919* (1963); A.S. Link, *Wilson. Campaigns for Progressivism and Peace, 1916-1917* (1965), pp. vii-viii.
3. Pierre Renouvin, 'Les Buts de guerre du gouvernement français', *Revue historique* (1966), pp. 1-34.
4. Christopher Andrew and A.S. Kanya-Forstner, 'The French Colonial Party and French Colonial War Aims 1914-1918', *The Historical Journal*, vol. XVII, pp. 79-106. Dr Andrew has also drawn my attention to the book by Kalervo Hovi, *Cordon sanitaire or barrière de l'est? The emergence of the new French Eastern European Alliance policy 1917-1919*. Annales Universitatis Turkuensis No. 135, 1975.
5. Guy Pedroncini, *Pétain, général en chef* (1974); Andre Kaspi, *Le temps des américains 1917-1918* (1976).
6. Raymond Poidevin, *Finances et relations internationales 1887-1914* (1970).
7. For Viviani's speech of 22 December 1914 see Georges Bonnefous, *Histoire politique de la Troisième République* (1957), vol. 2, pp. 57 ff.
8. See Maurice Paléologue, *La Russie des tsars pendant la guerre, 1921-1922*, vol. I, pp. 197-202, and Renouvin, 'Les buts de guerre du gouvernement', pp. 5-6.
9. This was also what Maurras thought. See Maurras to Barrès, 27 December 1914, in Maurice Barres, Charles Maurras *La République ou le Roi; Correspondance inédite 1888-1923* (1970), p. 545.
10. See Jean-Noel Jeanneney, *François de Wendel en République. L'Argent et le Pouvoir 1914-1940* (1976), pp. 33-5.
11. Abel Ferry, *Les Carnets secrets d'Abel Ferry 1914-1918* (1957), p. 573, quoted in Andrew and Kanya-Forstner, 'French Colonial War Aims'; G.H. Cassar, *The French and the Dardanelles* (1971), p. 58.
12. Rothwell, *British War Aims*, pp. 25-8.
13. This has been well studied by Dr D.J. Dutton in his unpublished thesis *France, England and the Politics of the Salonica Campaign* (PhD London, 1975). See also J.K. Tanenbaum, *Général Maurice Sarrail* (1974).
14. These and similar issues are studied in the unpublished thesis by H.D. Peiter, *Men of Good Will: French Businessmen and the First World War* (The University of Michigan, Ph.D., 1973). I am grateful to Mr. J.A. Neufeld of The London School of Economics for drawing my attention to this work.
15. For this ministerial circular of 27 August 1914 see Archives Nationales, Paris, F^{12} 7420. For replies to the circular see F^{12} 8197 and 8198.
16. An account of this conference and its implications is given by the Vicomte Georges d'Avenel, 'La Defense économique contre l'Allemagne', *Revue des Deux Mondes*, 1 August 1916, pp. 691 ff.
17. 3 and 10 December 1915. 'La Metallurgie francaise et le futur traite de paix.' Archives du Ministere des Affaires Etrangères, Paris. Series A. 1914-

20. Vol. 178.

18. Amongst other articles, see that by de Launay, "Le Problème Franco-Allemand du Fer", *Revue des Deux Mondes,* 15 July 1916, pp. 325 ff.

19. See the account of 'La Querelle de Briey' in Jeanneney, *François de Wendel en République,* pp. 65 ff. Marshal Joffre was probably correct when summing up this, and like, issues, he wrote 'Nous croyions tous que la guerre serait courte. à cet égard, tout le monde s'est trompé, civils et militaires, les strateges, les diplomates, les economistes et les financiers', (Joffre, *Mémoires* (1932), vol. 1, p. 123).

20. This was particularly organised by Gustave Tery in the newspaper *L'Oeuvre.*

21. The Pont-à-Mousson archives have been consulted by Charles S. Maier, *Recasting Bourgeois Europe* (1975), pp. 71-2.

22. R. Poincare, *Au service de la France. Neuf années de souvenirs* (1931), vol. VIII, pp. 8-9, quoted in Andrew and Kanya-Forstner, 'French Colonial War Aims', p. 86.

23. Archives du Ministère des Affaires Etrangères, Paris. Note sur l'état d'esprit des nationalites d'Autriche-Hongrie, 31 December 1914. Autriche-Hongrie vol. 149.

24. See Hovi, *Cordon sanitaire or barrière de l'est,* pp. 34-9.

25. By Pierre Renouvin, 'Les buts de guerre du gouvernement', p. 9.

26. Rothwell, *British War Aims,*pp. 70-3, 75; Briand's letter to Cambon is published in G. Suarez, *Briand, sa vie, son oeuvre* (1940), pp. 127-30.

27. Andrew Kaspi, *Le temps des américains 1917-1918,* pp. 140-1.

28. See the suggestion that Russia was becoming Germany's 'India'. Saint-Aulaire to the Foreign Minister, 16 December 1917. Archives du Ministere des Affaires Etrangères, Paris. Russia, vol. 667.

29. These matters are given detailed treatment in Hovi, *Cordon sanitaire or barrière de l'est.*

30. For the suggestion that Clemenceau abandoned both Palestine and Mosul to the British see Andrew and Kanya-Forstner, 'French Colonial War Aims', p. 104.

31. When, in February 1915, Kitchener was pressed to tell the French what plans he had in connection with Russia, he replied that 'owing to the rapid changes that take place on the political horizon in the Balkans and that part of the world, it seems difficult to see how any very fixed plan of action can be determined upon'. Quoted in John Gooch, *The Plans of War* (1974), p. 304.

SIR ROBERT BORDEN AND CANADA'S WAR AIMS

Robert Craig Brown

One of the more tiresome obligations of historians who write about
Canada's role in the Great War is to begin by belabouring the obvious:
'When Britain is at war', as Sir Wilfrid Laurier observed in 1910,
'Canada is at war.'[1] But that truism is an inadequate explanation of
Canada's commitment to the war effort, a commitment expressed in
Sir Robert Bordon's pledge, in the last hours of peace, that 'the Canadian people will be united in a common resolve to put forth every
effort and to make every sacrifice necessary to ensure the integrity and
maintain the honour of our Empire'.[2] Nor does it account for Canada's
two major war aims which the Borden Government believed were far
more important that the contemporary constitutional conventions of
the British Empire in 1914. The first, reflective of an era when Canadian politicians paid more than lip-service to high principles, was proclaimed by the Prime Minister in his speech to the House of Commons
during the hastily summoned war session of Parliament in August.

> Not for love of battle, not for lust of conquest, not for greed of
> possessions, but for the cause of honour, to maintain solemn pledges,
> to uphold the principles of liberty, to withstand forces that would
> convert the world into an armed camp; yea, in the very name of the
> peace that we sought at any cost save that of dishonour, we have
> entered into this war.[3]

The second war aim was to make clear to all who would notice, at home
and abroad, that Canada was not going to participate in the war as a
mere adjunct of the British Empire. The war would be an opportunity
to demonstrate Canada's resourcefulness and responsibility as an autonomous nation. The war effort would be a national war effort. The
Great War, as John Dafoe declared in the *Free Press* in Winnipeg, was
going to be 'Canada's War'.[4]

Compliance with constitutional convention offered Borden's Government the alternative of any number of limited commitments to the war
effort. However, to fight for the restoration of peace, for the cause of
honour, for the maintenance of solemn pledges, for the principles of

liberty, and for recognition of national status and stature required
more, much more. Nothing less than a total commitment was conso-
nant with such elaborate and ambitious war aims.

From the first to the very last days of the war Borden never
wavered in his conviction that Canada's contribution to the Great War
was disinterested and highly principled. Canada's soldiers, sailors and
airmen were fighting for 'the cause of freedom' and for 'the future des-
tiny of civilization and humanity'.[5] For Borden, a lawyer who believed that 'the chief insignia of a civilized nation are orderly government and respect for the law',[6] there was much more at stake than
territories that might be won or lost by the combatants. The principal
crime of the Kaiser and his military aristocracy was that their brutish
aggression undermined the foundations of all civilized societies,
crushed freedom, imposed bondage and threatened a world of chaos
and anarchy. Canada was fighting, Borden told an audience of distinguished lawyers in New York in 1916, 'to uphold public right, to pro-
mote the ends of what is known as international law'.[7]

Given the high-minded purposefulness of Canada's war effort, it
followed that Borden and his colleagues were unwilling to consider an
inconclusive peace settlement. The sword 'will not be sheathed until the
triumph of our cause is full and unmistakable', Borden declared in
1915.

> Whether the doctrine that might is right shall prevail and shall
> supersede the recognized canons of civilization, whether the creed of
> the jungle or the creed of Christianity shall inspire and guide
> humanity in the years to come — that is the issue forced upon the
> world in this war. To such a demand humanity can give but one
> answer, and Canada will do her part in making the answer complete
> and final.[8]

This determination put Borden at odds with another Dominion spokesman in the War Cabinet meetings of 1918. An Imperial General Staff
paper which looked forward to campaigns in both 1919 and 1920
caused General Smuts to wonder whether fighting the war out to the
bitter end was a reasonable policy for the Empire. 'I am very much
against fighting [the war] to the absolute end', said Smuts, 'because I
think that, although that end will be fatal to the enemy, it may possibly
be fatal to us too.'[9] Borden, who thought Smuts' speech 'left [him]
open to serious attack',[10] had no such doubts. He had already made his

position clear. 'We came over to fight in earnest; and Canada will fight it out to the end ... Let the past bury its dead, but for God's sake let us get down to earnest endeavour and hold this line until the Americans can come in and help us to sustain it till the end.'[11]

Similarly, the disinterested nature of Canada's war effort led Borden to express grave reservations about the territorial ambitions of his Empire colleagues when they discussed the disposition of captured German colonies. It was true that Sir Douglas Hazen, Canada's representative on the Territorial Disiderata Committee of the Imperial War Cabinet in 1917, had expressed a novel variant of Dominion territorial aspirations; he wanted not captured enemy colonies but allied lands! But Canada's support of the acquisition of St Pierre and Miquelon by Newfoundland and her interest in Greenland and in a cession of British Guiana to the United States in return for the Alaska panhandle were not pressing problems.[12] What were the ambitions of South Africa and especially Australia. 'Hughes wants to reach from one island to another across the Pacific', Borden sourly observed of the Australian Premier. 'He has very little vision beyond his own personal interests.'[13] 'So far as Canada is concerned,' Borden loftily told the Imperial War Cabinet, 'she did not go into the war in order to add territory to the British Empire.'[14]

On 22 August 1918, as the ship which brought Borden home from the Imperial War Cabinet meetings was approaching the port of New York, the Canadian Prime Minister spent a portion of the day catching up on his correspondence. The autumn offensive was already underway and the reports from the front were encouraging. He, of course, did not know that this was to be the final drive to victory. He still expected that the war would continue into 1919, perhaps even longer. But the news from the front, and especially reports handed to him just before he left London of the successful movements of the Canadian Corps, led him to reflect on the purpose and meaning of the Canadian war effort. 'The people of Canada entered this war from a profound conviction of duty to the Empire and to the civilized world', he wrote to L.S. Amery in London. 'Probably no part of the Britannic Commonwealth was more disinterested in reaching a decision as to that duty. We are ready to fight to the last for the cause as we understand it, for every reasonable safeguard against German aggression and for the peace of the world.'[15]

But the high principles motivating the Canadian war effort did not mean that Borden was prepared to accept the enormous sacrifice of his people's blood and treasure without any tangible reward. Quite the contrary. Because the Canadian contribution had been so great, because it had been so disinterested, Borden believed that his nation had an irrefutable claim to recognition as a principal combatant in its own right rather than as a subordinate part of the British Empire. It was an assumption he had made about his country's status in the Empire long before the war began. In fact, throughout his political career he argued that Canadian contributions to Imperial Defence had to be matched by a corresponding recognition of Canada's right to a voice in the counsels that determined the issues of war and peace. And the very magnitude of the Canadian war effort made it imperative that Canada's voice be recognised as that of a major combatant.

Throughout the early war years, of course, Canada was neither consulted about nor even informed of the vital policy decisions of the Imperial Government, much less given the 'right to an adequate voice in foreign policy and in foreign relations' that Borden demanded in Resolution IX of the 1917 Imperial War Conference.[16] Canadian Government orders were delayed at the Vickers' yard in Montreal while the company secretly assembled submarines for the British navy. The Admiralty, without consultation with Ottawa, requisitioned coastal vessels that were essential to domestic Canadian war production. The Government of Canada learned of the disposition of its soldiers from the same source as did the ordinary public of Canada, the censored daily press. Appeals for information were not answered; demands for consultation were side-stepped with a veneer of politeness. 'I fully recognize the right of the Canadian government to have some share of the control in a war in which Canada is playing so big a part,' the Colonel Secretary, Bonar Law, wrote in the fall of 1915. 'I am, however, not able to see any way in which this could be practically done . . . [and] if no scheme is practicable then it is very undesirable that the question should be raised.'[17]

Borden's frustration at these repeated demonstrations of the assumption of Canada's colonial status by London was revealed in his famous letter to Perley of 4 January 1916. Two paragraphs bear repeating:

> During the past four months since my return from Great Britain, the Canadian Government . . . have had just what information could be gleaned from the daily Press and no more. As to consultation, plans of campaign have been made and unmade, measures

adopted and apparently abandoned and generally speaking steps of
the most important and even vital character have been taken, post-
poned or rejected without the slightest consultation with the authorities of this Dominion.

It can hardly be expected that we shall put 400,000 or 500,000
men in the field and willingly accept the position of having no more
voice and receiving no more consideration than if we were toy
automata. Any person cherishing such an expectation harbours an
unfortunate and even dangerous delusion. Is this war being waged by
the United Kingdom alone, or is it a war waged by the whole Empire? If I am correct in supposing that the second hypothesis must
be accepted then why do the statesmen of the British Isles arrogate
to themselves solely the methods by which it shall be carried on in
the various spheres of warlike activity and the steps which shall be
taken to assure victory and a lasting peace?[18]

The 'toy automata' letter was never passed on to the British authorities
and no reply to Borden's question was forthcoming. But Borden knew
the answers well enough. The casual disregard of Canada's interests and
ambitions reflected the complacency of the first coalition government's
approach to the war. 'Procrastination, indecision, inertia, doubt, hesi-
tation and many other undesirable qualities have made themselves entirely too conspicuous in this war', he bitterly observed.[19] It was only
when the Lloyd George Government came to power that the situation
was righted. The new Prime Minister realised that the Dominions could
no longer be treated indifferently. 'We must have even more substantial
support from them before we can hope to pull through', he noted. 'It
is important that they should feel that they have a share in our councils
as well as in our burdens.'[20]

Even then the participation of the Dominion Prime Ministers in the
meetings of the Imperial War Cabinet of 1917 gave more form than substance of reality to the proclamation of the 'right to an adequate voice
in foreign policy' by the simultaneous meetings of the Imperial War
Conference. The deliberations of the War Cabinet were inconclusive and
soon after the disastrous Flanders offensive, with more than 15,000
Canadian casualties at Passchendaele, was sanctioned without consultation of the Canadian Government. The reversion 'to the old system of
communication',[21] as L.S. Amery put it, between the 1917 and 1918
meetings of the Imperial War Cabinet put the lie to Borden's grand
declaration, just as the 1917 meetings drew to a close, that Canada 'has

raised herself to the full rank and dignity of nationhood'.[22]

But not completely so. Lloyd George's Government might have had difficulty implementing its recognition of 'the full rank and dignity of nationhood' to Canada. Borden's Government, however, did not hesitate to assert its newly claimed posture. It did so in a manner even the most obtuse British official could not have missed. It had already created a Ministry of Overseas Military Forces of Canada charged with *negotiating* 'with His Majesty's Government, in all matters connected with the government command and disposition of the overseas forces of Canada'[23] and in June 1917, when Sir Julian Byng was assigned to other duties, the Canadians 'insisted' that Lieutenant-General Sir Arthur Currie be given command of the Canadian Corps.[24] Canadian soldiers henceforth would be commanded by a fellow citizen soldier from Canada; a Minister of Borden's Government would coordinate 'their operations and services with those of His Majesty's troops'.[25] From Ottawa's perspective, both were tangible symbols of nationhood. Still, the problem of consultation on high policy remained.

What made it worse in Borden's mind was the accumulating evidence of total incompetence in the British High Command. There was no justification for Passchendaele; no reason why the German spring offensive of 1918 should have been so successful. On a quiet Sunday afternoon in July 1918, Borden was having tea with the British Prime Minister at his country house. Lloyd George told him 'that for eight months he had been boiling with impotent rage against higher command, they had affiliations and roots everywhere.'[26] Borden was not impressed with Lloyd George's plight. Waving his finger before the British Prime Minister's eye, his voice shaking with anger, Borden replied that 'if ever there is a repetition of the battle of Passchendaele, not a Canadian soldier will leave the shores of Canada so long as the Canadian people entrust the government of their country to my hands.'[27]

This was the second occasion when Borden expressed his bitterness and anger about the war strategy of the Imperial Government. A month earlier the 1918 meetings of the Imperial War Cabinet had begun with a review by Lloyd George of the course of the war in the past year, including the continuing success of the German spring offensive. At the next meeting Borden, armed with devastating reports from General Currie which confirmed his worst fears of British incompetence, contemptuously compared the devotion to duty and earnest endeavour of the Canadian war effort with the 'lack of foresight, lack of preparation and . . . defects of system and organization' in the British High Command. He cited instance after instance where the bravery and sacrifice of his soldiers and their military successes had been undermined by British strategy. Currie, he said, had given him 'an awful picture of the war situation among the British. Says incompetent officers not removed, officers too casual, too cocksure.' Petty jealousies among the professional officers had held up the promotions of promising young men; it 'amounts to scrapping the brains of the nation in the greatest struggle in history'.[28]

This unexpected and shocking indictment of the British High Command, an indictment Lloyd George privately welcomed, led directly, within a week, to the creation of a Committee of Prime Ministers to 'share with the British Government, as far as can be arranged, the responsibility for the control of military operations in the future'.[29] Because this was the only occasion during the Great War when the Canadian Government had a role to play in strategic planning, it is worth pausing for a moment or two to examine the conclusions of the Prime Ministers' Committee.

Operations 'of the Passchendaele type', the Committee hoped, 'will never again be tolerated'. It was just this type of battle which gave the Committee grave doubts about the recommendation of the Chief of the Imperial General Staff, Sir Henry Wilson, for a general western offensive in the summer of 1919.

> The Committee agree that the Western front is the decisive front; they recalled, however, that the Western front has, so far, proved the doom of every attempt to reach a decision . . . Thus it appears to the Committee that the future operations on the Western front must turn to a considerable extent upon events in the East, the issue of which is not at present in sight. The Committee consider that no opportunity should be lost to direct the course of events in the East in such a manner as to embarrass the enemy and cause him to divert forces thither.

Clearly then, the politicians believed that a decision in the west in 1919, or in 1920, could only be achieved if there was a 'withdrawal of a substantial number of German divisions' to deal with 'a revitalized eastern front'.[30] And it was this conclusion that convinced Borden of the necessity of committing a Canadian force to the Siberian intervention.[31]

More important than the planning for future military operations and commitments was the principle of control of military strategy. About this the Prime Ministers' Committee had no doubts at all. 'The Government', they asserted, 'is ultimately responsible for the policy adopted.'

> ... it is not only the right, but the duty of the Government to assure itself that operations involving the possibility of heavy casualties are not embarked on unless they give a probability of producing commensurate results on the final issue of the war and without wrecking the future of the Empire. This does not mean that the Government should interfere in the conduct of military operations when once decided on, or hamper the higher Command in regard to minor operations for the rectification of the line, or the improvement of the tactical position; or that they should hamper it in taking advantage of any opportunity which may arise in the course of a battle for an effective counterstroke; but they have a right to insist that the general lines of major operations involving the possibility of a heavy casualty list are submitted for their approval ... The Government, indeed, is in the position of a board of Directors who have to insist that before committing the resources of the Company in some great enterprise, they shall be fully appraised of its prospects, cost, and consequence.[32]

The last sentence bears all the marks of Borden's influence. It certainly states the main point he, in support of Lloyd George, wanted to clarify in the Prime Ministers' Committee; the relationship between the roles of the politicians and the soldiers in military policy and planning. But even more important for the Canadian Prime Minister was the fact that his right to take part in such high level discussions of war policy as an equal had been recognised. Almost certainly that would not have happened had not Borden forced the formation of the Prime Ministers' Committee by his bitter but compelling denunciation of the high command in the Imperial War Cabinet.

That the war plans of the Prime Ministers' Committee were obviated by the sudden collapse of the enemy forces in the autumn of 1918 is of much less significance here than the opportunity imminent peace afforded for the consolidation of Canadian war aims. Logically it was an easy step from the right to a voice in war policy to an equally important role in planning for peace. In both cases, Borden argued, the right already had been won by the Canadian troops in the trenches. Whatever the constitutional impediments, however great the so-called practical difficulties the British bureaucrats imagined, they were of no significance whatever when measured alongside the splendid sacrifice of Canada's civilian soldiers. 'The press and people of this country take it for granted', Borden told Lloyd George just before he returned to England in the autumn of 1918, 'that Canada will be represented at the Peace Conference . . . New conditions must be met by new precedents.'[33]

Stating Canada's demand was one thing; getting it accepted was quite another. It took week after week of plodding persistent persuasion within the Imperial War Cabinet-British Empire Delegation to achieve a separate representation for Canada at the Peace Conference. At times the prospects were thoroughly discouraging and Borden wondered if it would not be better for Canada to strike out on her own. 'I am beginning to feel more and more that in the end, and perhaps sooner than later, Canada must assume full sovereignty', he wrote. 'She can give better service to G.B. and U.S. and to the world in that way.'[34] And as the weeks passed the letters from his Cabinet colleagues in Ottawa became more insistent. 'The people of Canada', wrote Newton Rowell, 'will not be content to have their Prime Minister occupy a subordinate position in relation to the Conference.'[35] The 'Canadian people', Sir Thomas White added, would not appreciate five American delegates throughout whole Conference and no Canadian entitled to sit throughout Conference nor would they appreciate several representatives from Great Britain and Canada none.'[36]

Eventually, Borden won out over the doubts of both British and Allied leaders. The Canadians had separate representation at the Conference and panel representation in the British Empire Delegation in the deliberations of the great Powers. Canada secured separate signatures for the peace treaties, separate representation in the League of Nations and the International Labour Organization, and the right, acknowledged in a statement drafted by Borden and signed by Lloyd George, Clemenceau and Woodrow Wilson on 6 May 1919, to membership in the League of Nations Council. With that it appeared that Canada's war aims had been achieved. Civilisation had been saved. A world organisation had been created which held out the prospect of upholding 'public right' and promoting 'the ends of what is known as international law'. Canada's status as an autonomous nation had been recognised.

It is intriguing to compare the roles of Canada and the mother country in the development of war policy and the enunciation of war aims. Professor Gooch has reminded us that Britain, to whom Canada looked for both leadership in war planning and direction in war objectives, could neither resolve the differences between her politicians and soldiers over strategic planning nor declare her war aims. And Borden, as we have seen, was dismayed and frequently disgusted by the failure of leadership and absence of direction in the British war effort. Canada, of course, save for Borden's membership in the Prime Ministers' Committee in the summer of 1918, took no part in the evolution of strategic policy during the war. However, Canada had unlimited freedom to criticise British policy and to articulate war aims of the most sweeping and ambitious character. Ironically, in light of Canada's aspirations for autonomy, that freedom was a luxury available only to a junior partner in the Imperial war effort.

As with other Government leaders in the Great War, the war was a chastening experience for the Canadian Prime Minister. By November 1918 the terrible toll of death among Canada's men in arms cast a grim, sombre pall over the war aims his government had so buoyantly proclaimed in the heady days of August, 1914. Quite properly, Sir Robert Borden was proud of his struggle to win international acknowledgement of Canada's autonomous status in the British Empire-Commonwealth. But when he wrote of it in January 1919 there was a note of bitterness in his words: 'Canada got nothing out of the war except recognition.'[37] Nor was Borden at all sure that even after the sacrifice of a generation of Canadians the preservation of civilisation was as secure as some believed. 'I have said that another such war would destroy our civilization', he recorded in his diary on the day the shooting stopped. 'It is a grave question whether this was may not have destroyed much that we regard as necessarily incidental thereto.'[38]

Notes

1.   *House of Commons Debates,* 12 January 1910, 1735.
2.   *Documents on Canadian External Relations (D.C.E.R.),* vol. I, p. 37.
3.   Cited, Henry Borden (ed.), *Robert Laird Borden. His Memoirs* (Toronto, 1938), vol. I. p. 461.
4.   Ramsay Cook, *The Politics of John W. Dafoe and the Free Press* (Toronto, 1963), p. 66.
5.   '"Canada at War", A Speech. . . by . . . Borden', 18 November 1916.
6.   Borden's speech to New England Society, New York, 22 December 1915.
7.   L.C. Christie Papers, 2, 1384-92. Speech draft.
8.   Borden Papers, Speech at Saint John, New Brunswick, 19 October 1915.
9.   Borden Papers, Imperial War Cabinet 31, Shorthand notes.
10. Borden Papers, Private, Diary, 14 August 1918.

11. Borden Papers, Imperial War Cabinet, 16 Shorthand notes.
12. Borden Papers, L.S. Amery to Borden, 19 August 1918 and Peace Conference file 18 (a), Amery to Borden,25 September 1918.
13. Borden Papers, Private, Diary, 29 January 1919.
14. Borden Papers, Imperial War Cabinet 44, Shorthand notes.
15. Borden Papers, Peace Conference file 18, Borden to Amery, 22 August 1918.
16. See R. Craig Brown and Robert Bothwell, 'The Canadian Resolution', in Michael Cross and Robert Bothwell (eds.), *Policy by Other Means. Essays in Honour of C.P. Stacey* (Toronto, 1973), pp. 165-78.
17. *D.C.E.R.,* vol. I, p. 96.
18. *Ibid.,* p. 104.
19. *Ibid.*
20. Lloyd George, *War Memoirs,* vol. IV, p. 1733.
21. *D.C.E.R.,* vol. I, p. 338.
22. Christie Papers,II, 3 Speech of 2 May 1917.
23. *D.C.E.R.,* vol. I, p. 148.
24. *Ibid.,* pp. 165-6.
25. *Ibid.,* p. 148.
26. Borden Papers, Private, Diary, 14 July 1918.
27. Henry Borden (ed.), *Letters to Limbo* (Toronto, 1971), p. vi.
28. Borden Papers, Imperial War Cabinet 16, Shorthand notes.
29. Borden Papers, Memoir Notes, August, 1918, Draft Report of the Prime Ministers' Committee.
30. *Ibid.*
31. On the Siberian intervention see J. Swettenham, *Allied Intervention in Russia, 1918-1919, and the Part Played by Canada* (Toronto, 1967); Gaddis G. Smith, 'Canada and the Siberian intervention, 1918-1919', *American Historical Review* (July 1959, pp. 866-77; and G.L. Cook, 'Sir Robert Borden, Lloyd George and British Military Policy, 1917-1918', *Historical Journal, 2 (1971).*
32. Borden Papers, Memoir Notes, August 1918, Draft Report of The Prime Ministers' Committee.
33. *D.C.E.R.,* vol. I, p. 218.
34. Borden Papers Private, Diary, 1 December 1918.
35. Borden Papers, Memoir Notes, Rowell to Borden, 24 Defemb4r 1918.
36. *D.C.E.R.,* vol. II, p. 23.
37. Borden Papers, Private, Diary, 13 January 1919.
38. *Ibid.,* 11 November 1918.

THE AMERICAN MILITARY AND STRATEGIC POLICY IN WORLD WAR I

Edward M. Coffman

My first thought upon being asked to give a paper on war aims and strategic policy in World War I was that there was little that I could say about the role of the American military in either. After all, war aims were tightly locked up in Woodrow Wilson's brain and the strategic parameters of the Great War were solidly in place by the time of the American intervention; hence one might assume that the army and navy had virtually nothing to do with either war aims or strategic policy. On second thought, however, I began to see possibilities in an explanation of why the services did not play a more significant role in formulating strategic policy in the early part of this century and in an attempt to analyse the evolution of the relationship between the American Army and the Allies in 1917-18.

In 1900, the navy established the General Board — the first permanent agency in the American military establishment for strategic planning. With the hero of Manila Bay, Admiral George Dewey, at its head, the Board made plans and recommended fleet movements and the location of bases. Although it could only advise, it was a significant departure from the ad hoc committees organised to consider specific problems in the past.[1]

Three years later, Congress created the General Staff and gave the army its planning agency. Throughout the period up to World War I, however, the lack of understanding as to the proper duties of the General Staff combined with the paucity of trained staff officers hampered the development of this crucial body. A Field Artillery Major who served on the General Staff from 1911 to 1913 concisely described the situation.

> Most of the General Staff officers then were of the type whose conception of their job was to get to their desks at 9 A.M., pass papers from the 'In' basket to the 'Out' basket, read the Army and Navy Journal, and gossip about army politics. Their tendency was to concern themselves too much with administrative matters and too little with high planning and original thinking.[2]

A month before the General Staff became operative in 1903, the service secretaries established the Joint Board which they hoped would serve to co-ordinate army and navy planning. This board which met monthly was supposed to pass judgement upon already prepared plans and projects. Henry Breckinridge who was Assistant Secretary of War from 1913 to 1916 gave an indication of the importance of this board when he recalled: 'This was a board I fooled with on hot summer afternoons when there was nothing else to do.'[3]

Although the United States had the institutions for strategic planning for more than a decade prior to World War I, their effectiveness was limited. In addition to reasons previously cited, the attitudes and prejudices of serving officers and, most of all, the relationship of these organisations to the President and the State Department — the makers of foreign policy — were influential in shaping the course of strategic planning.

The single most prestigious military man who took part in this planning was Admiral Dewey who headed the General Board from its establishment until his death in January 1917. Although one might assume the concern of American naval strategists with the defence of the Philippines and the control of the Caribbean, it might be a surprise to learn of the large place Germany played in their thinking. Dewey's most recent biographer noted that the admiral 'was strongly — almost fanatically — anti-German'.[4] The fear of an aggressive Germany, ambitious for a greater empire, apparently haunted other naval officers as well. Ironically, at this time, the so-called more progressive army officers were coming under extensive German influence. Many of their textbooks at the staff school at Fort Leavenworth were translated from the original German. Always more concerned with the problems of raising and training forces, rather than the larger question of against whom and where these forces would be used, these officers were greatly impressed with German military methods. The attitude of two such well-trained staff officers worried their brigade commander in June 1917. En route to France, he confided to his diary: 'The impression that the average man derives from hearing them talk . . . is the hopelessness, the utter folly of our resisting or fighting the Germans at all.'[5] At least one of this progressive group of Leavenworth graduates was not as impressed by the Germans in person. When Captain George Van Horn Moseley attended the German and French manoeuvres in 1912, he was put off by the 'cold attitude of the German officer toward the outsider, especially the American Army officer'. On the other hand, he found French officers 'anxious to assist us . . . and to show us every courtesy'.[6]

The basic limitation in the military's role in formulating strategic policy stemmed from the American tradition of civil-military relations. If there was to be a regular military establishment (and there were always some Americans who denied the need for such an institution), it would be clearly understood that the civil authority was dominant. This belief, certainly justifiable and worthwhile in itself, came to have damaging ramifications through its interpretation. Unless in an actual state of war, Americans expected their military men to be silent and, generally, as inconspicuous as possible. As Woodrow Wilson's first Secretary of State, William Jennings Bryan, bluntly phrased it at a cabinet meeting in May 1913: ' . . . the military could not be trusted to say what could or couldn't be done 'till we actually got into war.'[7] This clear-cut distinction between civil and military roles meant, in fact, an isolation of the two in peace-time when each often acted in common areas without reference to the other. The foreign policy makers thus would not take into consideration the military aspects of their problems and actions while the military planners had little or no information, much less guidance, from the diplomats and political leaders in planning for potential conflicts.[8]

In the period 1913-17, President Wilson and Secretary of the Navy, Josephus Daniels, were particularly suspicious of military men and strove earnestly to keep them in subordination. As for foreign policy, in those complex, difficult days, Wilson apparently had little regard for any advice from military leaders. From them he evidently expected only obedience. Within three months of his inauguration in 1913, he threatened, with the approval of Secretary Daniels, to abolish the General Board and the Joint Board because he thought they were overstepping their bounds.[9] The Secretary of War, Lindley M. Garrison, incidentally, was much more sympathetic towards the military. This attitude led to friction with the President and eventually in 1916 to Garrison's resignation.

An incident in the autumn of 1915 illustrates Wilson's lack of understanding of the function of military planners and their potential value. The President, 'trembling and white with passion', pointed out to Acting Secretary of War Henry Breckinridge, a short item in the Baltimore *Sun* which read: 'It is understood that the General Staff is preparing a plan in case of war with Germany.' He told Breckinridge to investigate and determine the truth of this report. If it was true, he further instructed the Acting Secretary 'to relieve at once every officer of the General Staff and order him out of Washington'.[10]

Despite the distrust and naïveté of the President, military planners continued to work — albeit unrealistically and virtually in a policy vacuum. The General Board evolved the Orange and Black plans for possible war with Japan and Germany, respectively, and the General Staff developed offensive plans against Canada and Mexico and defensive plans to counter attacks by Japan, Britain, and Germany.

When war did come in Europe, it is an indication of the American army's readiness that the Chief of Staff of the Eastern Department at Governor's Island in New York harbour wrote a friend at the Army War College on 1 August 1914: 'We are without European maps and without funds to buy them at this headquarters . . . you will probably have some maps at the War College from which you might send us a few. If so, please do so at once.'[11]

The desire of military men to prepare for the possibility of war clashed with the President's interpretation of neutrality. 'We must be impartial in thought as well as in action', Wilson told Congress in August 1914.[12] Those officers who publicly advocated preparations soon learned of the President's ire. He attempted to silence former Chief of Staff Leonard Wood while Secretary Daniels told Rear-Admiral Bradley A. Fiske, after he read Fiske's article on preparedness: 'You cannot write or talk any more; you can't even say that two and two make four.'[13]

How could an officer not think about what he read in the newspapers of the tremendous struggle raging in Europe? How could any self-respecting officer not wonder about what it might mean to the United States?

Hugh A. Drum, a bright young staff officer with the expedition in Vera Cruz, Mexico, wrote a prescient letter to his wife on 4 August 1914:

> It is terrible to think of the affairs of Europeans. The loss of life will be immense and [the] result of this war will be hard to predict. Germany will have a hard time unless she can win in the first few months. If the war lasts for a long period Germany must lose and may disappear as a nation. The world will blame her & she no doubt deserves the blame.

But Drum did not anticipate the American intervention nor could he know the significant role he would play in the American Expeditionary Forces.[14]

The President's strong stand against what he would construe as military meddling in foreign policy naturally inhibited planners; yet there was another reason why the army and the navy did not devote more official consideration to the European war. From 1911 until the spring of 1917, American interest in the unsettled affairs of Mexico brought about troop concentrations on the border and, in 1914 and 1916, two invasions by American forces. Although there was no formal declaration of war (which incidentally made the inflexible army plan useless when the Americans seized Vera Cruz since the actual situation did not conform to the premise of the planners), the tension caused by events and the possibility of a general war with Mexico permeated military thinking in this period.[15]

From the sinking of the *Lusitania* in May 1915, until the United States entered the war two years later, many Americans were captivated by the Preparedness Movement. Although the movement was instigated by the European war and would wax and wane, to a certain extent, according to the events of that war, Preparedness advocates generally did not endorse intervention. What they wanted to prepare for was a unilateral defence against the victor. This provided an opportunity for the army to plan for mobilisation, yet still stay within the limits set by the President's neutrality stance and his refusal to provide any guidance as to potential enemies. Thus, in 1915 and 1916, army leaders were concerned with such questions as the place of the National Guard in any defence scheme and whether or not they should use volunteering or conscription to raise a large force in future emergencies. They wanted a Federal reserve and conscription but obviously Congress would have to approve such drastic changes in the nation's military system. As it happened Congress refused to support the army on both points.[16] It did, however, provide in 1916 for an incremental build-up of the regular army over a period of five years. The legislators also supported a large naval building programme.

In early 1917, the German unrestricted submarine campaign made conflict with the United States virtually inevitable. This is not to say that a majority of Americans supported intervention or that their leaders grasped the ramifications of a declaration of war. In the War Department, during those three months before the American entry, there were periods of uncertain calm as men pondered the future. On 10 February Major-General Tasker H. Bliss, the Assistant Chief of Staff, wrote a fellow general:

> Notwithstanding our official relations with Germany (perhaps it is
> better to say, lack of official relations) things are going along very
> quietly here. It does not seem to have given any additional vitality to
> the question of training, universal or otherwise. At any rate, it does
> not look as though anything would [will] be done until we are
> literally forced to do so. Even then it may be that they will rely
> entirely on the Navy.[17]

Planning continued nevertheless. Since so much attention had been paid
to manpower mobilisation, it is not surprising that the mobilisation plan
would be realistic. By mid-February, the Chief of Staff had in his hands
a detailed plan for raising, equipping, quartering, and training an army
of four million.[18] The General Staff assumed in this plan the premise
of conscription. Although President Wilson endorsed the concept, it
would be mid-May before Congress passed the Selective Service Act.

In this twilight period, just before the United States became a belli-
gerent, General Staff officers considered three suggestions, involving
expeditions to Europe. Of these two now seem not only irrelevant but
also bizarre. The military attaché in Greece proposed a landing in Mace-
donia with the purpose of taking Bulgaria out of the war which in turn,
he presumed, would lead to the collapse of Turkey and, by releasing
Allied forces in that theatre, give the Allies more strength on the
Western Front. The Chief of Staff, Major-General Hugh L. Scott,
initiated the second proposal of landing an expedition in neutral
Holland to strike at the Germans behind the Western Front. In both
cases, the United States could act independently of the Allies. In this
regard the chief legal officer of the army, Major-General Enoch H.
Crowder, wrote a friend on 28 February: 'I am utterly and irreconcil-
ably opposed to your view that we should join the Allies and make
peace in common with them. A thousand times 'NO' to this proposition.
Our case is stronger than theirs, and we do not want to divide the
strength of our position with anybody.'[19] It was a point of view that
Woodrow Wilson and many other Americans would have found con-
genial.

On 27 March, six days before the President asked Congress for a
declaration of war, General Bliss called upon the General Staff to make
an estimate as to how long it would take to send half a million troops to
France. The War College Division, which handled war plans in the

General Staff, reported back in four days that the army would require two years and two months to develop a force of that size and transport it to Europe.[20]

Despite the floating of ideas about various expeditions within the War Department, there were no real plans to send a sizable force abroad when Congress declared war on 6 April. Indeed, most military and political leaders assumed that the American contribution would be loans and perhaps some naval support. In late March, President Wilson had endorsed the latter and dispatched Rear-Admiral William S. Sims to London to effect co-ordination with the British. The advice that Chief of Naval Operations William S. Benson gave Sims, who was a well-known Anglophile, indicates the difficulty of coalition warfare. 'Don't let the British pull the wool over your eyes. It is none of our business pulling their chestnuts out of the fire. We would as soon fight the British as the Germans.'[21]

Regardless of individual preferences, the United States was at war on the same side with the British and the French. In late April missions from those nations arrived in Washington eager to influence the American effort. Although both groups perhaps surprised their hosts with requests for manpower, Marshal Joseph Joffre, the Hero of the Marne, made the best impression when he asked for a division to show the flag and boost the morale. In addition to Joffre's personal appeal, the General Staff had received three studies originated in different elements of the French Army. Only one recommended dispatch of a division and held out the possibility of a combat role for American units. The others concentrated on the need for labourers, technicians and service troops.[22] The British also asked for support troops and broached the touchy subject of using individual American replacements to fill their depleted ranks. President Wilson personally approved Joffre's request for a division. One of the three staff officers designated to work up the plan for this division later recalled: 'It is characteristic of our situation at that time that we did not have a single formed division in the American regular army. We therefore had to extemporize one.'[23]

The French had won the first round in the contest between the Allies for American manpower. When the British military representative attempted to counter Joffre's appeal by pointing out the advantages of having American soldiers associating with people who spoke the same language, Secretary of War Newton D. Baker closed the subject by saying that in all likelihood the first expeditionary force would co-operate with the French.[24] Throughout 1917, the Army worked almost

entirely with the French while the Navy, during the entire war, would
be thrown in for the most part with the British. The reason for the
latter — the dominance among the Allies of British seapower — is more
obvious and more simple than the causes for the former.

In August 1917, the Chief of the British Secret Service in the
United States wrote an analysis on Anglo-American relations. In this
memorandum Sir William Wiseman correctly gauged the views of the
Americans. He emphasised that they saw themselves as disinterested
arbitrators rather than allies. As for co-operation with the British and
the French, he commented:

> There still remains a mistrust of Great Britain, inherited from the
> days of the War of Independence, and kept alive by the ridiculous
> history books still used in the national schools. On the other hand,
> there is the historical sympathy for France.[25]

Aside from these traditional attitudes, there were current realities
which made the French case more logical to the Americans. The
Western Front was mostly in France and the French had carried the
major part of the burden there. The collapse of the Nivelle offensive
and the decline in French morale simply emphasised the French appeal.
In this regard, however, neither the Americans nor, perhaps, Joffre and
his aides were aware of the full extent of the disastrous effects on the
morale of the French army.[26]

During May, the War Department attempted to carry out its promise
to the French. Secretary of War Newton D. Baker selected a commander for the expedition — John J. Pershing — who then gathered a
nucleus staff while the General Staff put together his initial command.
On 28 May the day Pershing and his staff sailed, the General Staff
received an infuriating message to the effect that the French General
Staff wanted only service troops in the initial contingent. Of course, at
this time, plans for the transportation of the First Division were far
advanced. The Acting Chief of Staff, Tasker H. Bliss, presumably somewhat exasperated, commented: ' . . . General Pershing's expedition is
being sent abroad on the urgent insistence of Marshal Joffre and the
French Mission.' It was up to the French to make suitable arrangements
for these combat troops. Bliss suspected an ulterior motive in this
message. 'They evidently think that, having yielded to the demand for a
small force for *moral* effect it is to be quite soon followed by a large
force for *physical* effect.' He added: 'Thus far we have made no plans

for this.' Indeed a few days later a General Staff document stated that
if the rate of transportation of this initial force of 25,000 was to be
continued it would take seven years to put a million men in France.[27]

American leaders made another basic strategic decision in May 1917.
Although the General Staff had earlier considered expeditions to other
theatres and similar projects would come up again, the Secretary of War
and his military advisers were adamantly opposed to such ideas. The
French and British missions emphasised the significance of the Western
Front and the Americans agreed. Secretary Newton D. Baker recalled:
' . . . General Pershing, General Scott, General Bliss and I had agreed
that the war would have to be won on the western front at the time
General Pershing started overseas. At one of our conferences before he
left we discussed some of the sideshows and decided that they were all
useless . . . '[28]

President Wilson delegated extraordinary authority to Pershing. If
one considers his feelings toward military men, this might seem odd;
however, it was in keeping with his attitude toward the separation of
civil and military matters. This was war and soldiers waged war. Secretary Baker was in full sympathy with this approach as was the Acting
Chief of Staff. Major-General Bliss, who by rank and position was
Pershing's superior officer, might have taken a stronger stance but he
downgraded his own position to that of an assistant to Pershing's Chief
of Staff.[29] (The latter in the summer of 1917 was a lieutenant-colonel.)
Later this would cause some difficulties when Peyton C. March, a
stronger individual who held the office in higher regard, became Chief
of Staff. But Baker set the scene at the very beginning when he told
Pershing that he would not interfere, as he put it, 'with his administration of military questions or permit them to be interfered with by my
military associates on this side'. This meant that the basic decisions and
the planning as to the future development of the American Expeditionary Forces were Pershing's responsibility. As the first step in this
direction Secretary Baker suggested to the President (who approved)
that future planning await Pershing's observations and recommenda-
tions. At the time he wrote this letter — 8 May — Baker had never even
met Pershing.[30]

On the voyage to Europe, Pershing put his staff to work on requisite
plans for an AEF of one million men. While he did the honours in
London, he sent ahead a staff committee to inspect ports and railroads
to prepare a recommendation as to a line of communications for his
army. What these officers discovered as did, a few days later, another

Staff committee which studied the question of which sector the AEF
would occupy, was that the French had made their own decisions and
had already begun preparations. Thus at St Nazaire the first committee
found the French putting up barracks for the Americans. Accompanied
by a French officer, significantly a descendant of Lafayette, the second
group visited towns which the French had selected as training centres
for the infantry and artillery and even an observation post where they
could see the front line sector chosen for them by the French. In their
report, they noted that ' . . . the French authorities had formulated a
definite plan for the location and partial training of the American
forces'. And they recommended accepting this plan.[31]

In his memoirs, Pershing explained at length why he chose this particular sector near the eastern end of the Western Front in Lorraine
which meant that the American Expeditionary Forces would have
French troops on both flanks. He pointed out that logistical facilities
would not sustain the large AEF that he envisioned in the British sector.
Besides, he said, they were primarily concerned with the protection of
the Channel ports. He could not insert the AEF between the British and
French since that would displace French troops positioned to protect
Paris. This then left him only the choice of a sector within the French
line. The specific area he selected, he pointed out, provided the proper
terrain in which he could use the AEF as a manoeuvre force to crack the
stalemate. His reasoning made sense; however, he failed to mention that
the French had laid the foundation for this plan. He merely stated that
'We were generally committed to operate with or near the French when
our army should be ready'.[32]

When the First Division arrived, its training, according to Pershing,
'was left almost wholly to the direction of the French'. By September
the dominance of the French was beginning to pall. A member of
Pershing's staff, Hugh Drum, confided in his diary: ' . . . we do not need
this help any longer.' The French were too defensive-minded for their
American protégés. A few weeks later, Drum complained again: 'The
French are still trying to handle us and train our troops. It is funny that
they cannot see the necessity for our paddling our own Canoe.'[33]

In a strategic study which Drum and two other officers prepared for
Pershing in September they acknowledged that the AEF would co-
operate 'especially with the French' and noted that American public
opinion favoured this course. They also predicted difficulties in Russia
and on the Italian front and prophesised that the Germans would
launch a 'serious' offensive against the French in the spring. They did

not believe that either the French or the British would stage a decisive offensive in 1918. The AEF, with the help of the French they thought, would be able to clear the St Mihiel in the coming year and in 1919 would be 'a decisive force' in the campaigning.[34]

Until the autumn of 1917, the British could afford to take a casual view of the American reinforcement. Certainly, any help was welcome but there did not appear to be a pressing need. After all, Field Marshal Sir Douglas Haig might strike the decisive blow in one of his offensives. Besides, as late as 31 October there were only 87,000 Americans in France.[35] The collapse of Russia, the disastrous defeat of the Italians, and the failure of Haig's attacks combined to make the necessity of American manpower obvious.

During the months of November through January, there was a marked shift in the British attitude toward the virtual monopoly the French had maintained over the use of American troops. The revelation of their own severe manpower shortages and the fear of German offensives in the coming year caused British leaders to seek Americans to help bolster their end of the Western Front. The French naturally still wanted the Americans in their camp. Their disasters had been in the spring so the various Allied failures in the autumn merely compounded their fears. Yet the British had a trump to play in this deadly serious game — shipping. They had definitely begun to win the battle for the sea-lanes; thus it would be feasible to transport large numbers of American troops across the Atlantic and they had the ships.

As the Allied leaders met in the recently organised Supreme War Council and under other auspices, all were aware of the German threat. The French and the British pressed the American leaders in the United States as well as Pershing to supply small combat units to be incorporated into their larger commands. Although Pershing was adamant about the development of an independent and eventually decisive AEF, he recognised the possibilities of a *quid pro quo* agreement with the British.

On 1 January 1918, Pershing's chief of staff ordered a staff study made 'of the best place to employ the AEF on the Western front'. He told the planners: 'Heretofore we have approached this subject on the understanding that we were limited to some secteur [sic] far enough to the east to permit the employment of much of the French Armies between the AEF and the BEF. Without that limitation please now study the question.' He added that the Operations Section should also consider the possibility that 'the British might be induced with their own shipping to land at Channel ports one or more [divisions] ... to be trained in areas already prepared behind the present B.E.F. lines.'[36]

Within a week, Fox Conner, the Chief of the Operations Section, had completed the study. In contrast with the strategic study of late September, his estimate was that the Germans would launch two offensives against the French and a limited attack against the British. In regard to the relationship with the Allies, he recalled: 'We once decided to be more intimately associated on land with the French than with the British.' This was not an inflexible decision, however. A shift of American forces to the British would benefit British morale but at the possible cost of French morale. He concluded that it would be best to continue the present plan. As for the British, Colonel Conner recommended that they 'should be plainly told that our ability to conduct an offensive in 1919 depends on increasing the rate of transporting, equipping and homogeneously training our troops in such a way as not to fritter them away.' If the British accede to this, the Americans would permit them to transport and supply 'a certain number of complete divisions' to be placed in the rear of the British line. Conner believed that this should not be done, however, 'without at least the passive consent of the French'.[37]

It was a rather arrogant stance for a very junior member of the coalition to take but it was one with which John J. Pershing agreed wholeheartedly. His comment in this paper was that he and Pétain had 'practically decided' on the American sector's location (between St Mihiel and Pont-à-Mousson); that he expected to extend the line of this sector in both directions; and finally that 'we should begin to make plans to carry out necessary construction leading up to what is to become the American sector'.[38]

During January Pershing met with the Chief of the Imperial General Staff, Sir William Robertson, to discuss the transportation and distribution of American troops. He also talked with other French and British leaders including the commander of the French Army, Philippe Pétain and Prime Minister David Lloyd George. At the Supreme War Council session at Versailles on 29 January Sir Maurice Hankey, Secretary of the Imperial War Cabinet, commented: 'Much misunderstanding because Pershing wanted the troops attached mainly for training, though willing that they should do their share of the fighting, while Robertson wanted them mainly for fighting, though willing that they should be trained.'[39] Robertson wanted battalions to build up the depleted British divisions. Pershing held fast for the transportation of

complete divisions. In the end his obstinacy won since the British
needed men anyway they could get them. They agreed to bring six
divisions but all of the troops except the artillery would train with
Haig's army.[40]

This agreement made available the British tonnage which would play
such a key role in the tremendous troop movements of the next
months. At this time, 31 January,there were only 216,00 men in the
AEF. In April 116,000 made the Atlantic crossing and in the remaining
six months, another million and a half.[41] These figures were only
visions — optimistic ones at that — in January and February for Allied
leaders. They had difficulty seeing beyond the awesome threat of the
German offensives they expected to come in the spring.

When the Germans did make their move in March and smashed a
British army, both Allies stepped up their appeals for American aid.
Pershing was willing to let them use the troops available but he baulked
at any plan which he thought would interfere with the ultimate goal of
an independent AEF. The British went over his head and made an
agreement — ships for men — in Washington only to have Secretary of
War Baker renege when Pershing complained. In turn, the American
General negotiated what he considered more favourable terms with the
British Secretary of War.[42]

Premier Georges Clemenceau was irritated when he arrived at the
Supreme War Council meeting on 1 May. Not only had the British
continued to play an increasingly important role in dealing with the
Americans to the extent of leaving the French out of recent negotiations — but also, in his view, the British were being too generous with
Pershing. The war could be lost while the Allies waited for Pershing to
build up his army without apparent regard for the currently desperate
situation. As the aged 'Tiger of France' walked to the meeting with Sir
William Wiseman, he voiced his resentment.

> He was talking in his way — joking but serious — about Lloyd
> George. He thought that Lloyd George only understood the situation
> in a general way. As we passed a butcher shop, he stopped and
> pointed with his cane to a sheep hanging in the shop. 'See, that's
> Lloyd George. The sheep has eight hearts and ten livers; and he
> wants to give them all away. Pershing is getting all of the meat. I
> want some of the meat.[43]

In those two days of emotion-charged meetings, the French and British leaders did all they could to convince the American Commander-in-Chief of the danger of his clinging to his goal at such a precarious time. But the tough Missourian withstood their efforts. Although he relented to the extent of approving for one month a previous troop shipment agreement, he forced a formal acknowledgement of an independent AEF. Secretary Baker supported his commander in his stand. On 7 May Baker analysed the confrontations at Allied conferences in a letter to his friend, General Tasker H. Bliss, the American military representative on the Supreme War Council.

> There is just a little disposition on the part of both British and French to feel that they are in a position to demand, or at least to insist, upon the fulfilment of expectations on their part as against a right on the part of the United States to pursue its own policy. For this reason I am very glad that we have from the first insisted upon leaving these questions to the discretion of General Pershing . . . [44]

There would be other conferences and further agreements but the American victory in the regimental assault at Cantigny in late May, the showing American troops made in the fighting near Château-Thierry, and, most of all, the huge increase in the American reinforcements changed the situation drastically. In mid-July, the French and the Americans stopped the last German offensive within a day; then, three days later on 18 July they staged a counter-attack near Soissons which was, in fact, a turning of the tide. During that month 306,000 Americans crossed the Atlantic. To place that figure in perspective, Pershing had only some 318,000 in the entire AEF on 31 March.[45]

As his command increased in strength and confirmed his faith in its fighting prowess, Pershing was quicker to show resentment at what he construed to be patronising. On 31 May, he told off the French High Commissioner: 'Gave Mr. [André] Tardieu some of my ideas on the attitude of French in trying to lead us about too much by the hand and their disposition to occupy themselves too much with our affairs.' He also noted in his diary Tardieu's reaction: 'He seemed just a little surprised.'[46] In those months during which the American role steadily expanded, Pershing cooperated with the Allies and accepted the authority of the recently appointed supreme commander, Ferdinand Foch, but on his own terms.

Premier Clemenceau, who found it difficult to accept the fact that President Wilson had delegated so much power to a soldier, did not hold Pershing in high regard. As late as October, he tried to have the American removed from command. Nevertheless, the newly formed American First Army's victory at St Mihiel and its hard fighting in the Meuse-Argonne campaign served the French and, indeed, the Allied cause as Foch realised — evidently more so than his premier.

The British were not altogether pleased with Pershing either. Lloyd George complained on 14 July, 'we must have more American divisions to train in our lines. They had come in our ships and we were entitled to them.' In the end he did get ten American divisions to train with the BEF and two stayed to fight as a separate corps for the remainder of the war.[47]

The war ended on 11 November so there was no need for the great offensive in the spring of 1919 on which American plans had focused. If there had been, Pershing apparently expected to be the commander. In early October he told a staff officer that when the AEF had more men on line than the French or the British then 'command should go to an American'.[48]

The place of American military men had certainly changed from the limbo to which their political masters had relegated them up to the declaration of war. A retired officer who had been instrumental in the creation of the General Staff summed up the situation in a letter to Pershing only a few days before the end of the war: 'What a wonderful thing it is to see a war run by military men instead of politicians.'[49] After being excluded from the corridors of power, they had come virtually to monopolise what Allied leaders construed to be political as well as military affairs. Grand strategy, as it were. In part, this was the result of Woodrow Wilson's personal attitude toward soldiers and war. Yet, Wilson's interpretation could fit easily into the American civil-military tradition of the enhancement of the professional military in war and its deflating to the point of obscurity in peace.

As an epilogue, I would like to add one last comment on the American-Allied relationship. I have perhaps dwelled too much on the level of Pershing and his staff so I shall give another, albeit similar, viewpoint. In 1960, I asked a former chief of the AEF Air Service, Benjamin D. Foulois, about co-ordination with the Allies. He answered with a story about the chief of staff of the Second Division — Preston Brown.

Shortly before the jump-off at St. Mihiel, a young lieutenant, 24 or so, came to his headquarters from GHQ. He asked: 'Is there anything I can do for you?' P. Brown answered: 'Since we've been here, we've had to fight the British, French, Italians, and Belgians before we could fight the Germans. You can get the hell out of here.'[50]

Notes

1. In recent years three excellent studies which deal with the General Board in varying degree have appeared. John A.S. Grenville and George B. Young, *Politics, Strategy and American Diplomacy: Studies in Foreign Policy, 1873-1917* (New Haven, Conn., 1966); Richard D. Challener, *Admirals, Generals, and American Foreign Policy: 1898-1914* (Princeton, N.J., 1973); and Ronald Spector, *Admiral of the New Empire: The Life and Career of George Dewey* (Baton Rouge, La., 1974).

2. William Lassiter, 'Memoir', U.S. Military Academy Library, West Point, N.Y. In World War I, Lassiter became a major general and a chief of corps artillery.

3. Henry Breckinridge interview, 12 November 1958.

4. Spector, *Admiral of the New Empire*, p. 82.

5. Robert L. Bullard, *Personalities and Reminiscences of the War* (Garden City, N.Y., 1925), p. 33. For an excellent discussion of the Leavenworth schools in this era, see Timothy K. Nenninger, 'The Fort Leavenworth Schools: Postgraduate Military Education and Professionalization in the U.S. Army, 1880-1920' (PhD dissertation, University of Wisconsin, 1974).

6. George Van Horn Moseley, 'One Soldier's Journey', 109-119, Moseley Papers, Library of Congress.

7. Spector, *Admiral of the New Empire*, p. 194.

8. Finally in 1938, President Franklin D. Roosevelt approved the creation of a standing liaison committee of State, War, and Navy Departments officers to provide regular co-ordination. See pages 89-91 in Mark S. Watson, *The War Department: Chief of Staff: Prewar Plans and Preparations* (Washington, D.C., 1950) in the *United States Army in World War II* series.

9. E. David Cronon (ed.), *The Cabinet Diaries of Josephus Daniels, 1913-1921* (Lincoln, Neb., 1963), p. 68.

10. As it happened, nothing came of this except Breckinridge's warning to planners to 'camouflage' their work. The acting Chief of Staff, Tasker H. Bliss, wrote this incident up in a memo which appears on pages 106-107 in Frederick Palmer, *Bliss, Peacemaker: The Life and Letters of General Tasker Howard Bliss* (New York, 1934). In my interview with him in 1958, Mr Breckinridge confirmed this story.

11. William G. Haan to Charles Crawford, 1 August 1914, William G. Haan Papers, Box 2. State Historical Society of Wisconsin, Madison, Wisconsin.

12. Arthur Walworth, *Woodrow Wilson* (New York, revised edition, 1965), vol. I, p. 407.

13. Bradley A. Fiske, *From Midshipman to Rear-Admiral* (New York, 1919), pp. 595-6.

14. Drum to wife, 4 August 1914, Hugh A. Drum Papers in possession of Hugh Drum Johnson, Closter, New Jersey.

15. Challener, *Admirals, Generals*, pp. 344-63, 379-97.

16. Not all army leaders, of course, were for conscription but the Chief of

Staff and several of the most influential ones were. Secretary of War
Garrison and Assistant Secretary Breckinridge resigned over the Federal
reserve issue. The best account of the Preparedness Movement is John P.
Finnegan, *Against the Specter of a Dragon: The Campaign for American
Military Preparedness, 1914-1917* (Westport, Conn., 1974).

17.   Bliss to George Bell, 10 February 1917, Letterbook 209, Tasker H. Bliss
Papers, Library of Congress.

18.   Joseph E. Kuhn to the Chief of Staff, 14 February 1917, WCD 9876-20 in
War Department Historical File 7-31, Record Group 165 National Archives.

19.   Crowder to William G. Haan, 28 February 1917, Box 3, Haan Papers.
These two plans are analysed in Ronald Spector, 'You're Not Going to
Send Soldiers Over There Are You!'. The American Search for an alter-
native to the Western Front 1916-1917', *Military Affairs*, vol. XXXVI,
No. 1 (February 1972), pp. 1-4.

20.   Bliss to J.E. Kuhn, 27 March 1917, Letterbook 210; and Bliss Memo,
31 March 1917, Letterbook 211, Bliss Papers.

21.   As quoted in David F. Trask, *Captains and Cabinets: Anglo-American
Naval Relations, 1917-1918* (Columbia, Mo., 1972), p. 55. For state of
War Department planning see Memo for the Adjutant General, 6 April
1917 WCD 6291-18 in W.D. Historical File 7-31, RG 165 NA.

22.   The French Plans – two from the General Staff and one from General
Nivelle – are summarised in Chief of the Military Mission, Paris, to Chief of
the Army War College, 18 April 1917, WCD 10050-2, W.D. Historical File
7-31, RG 165 NA.

23.   John M. Palmer, *Washington, Lincoln, Wilson: Three War Statesmen*
Garden City, N.Y., 1930), p. 322.

24.   Frederick Palmer, *Newton D. Baker: America at War,* 2 vols. (New York,
1931), vol. I, pp. 154-5.

25.   W.B. Fowler, *British-American Relations, 1917-1918: The Role of Sir
William Wiseman* (Princeton, N.J. 1969), p. 249.

26.   James G. Harbord, *The American Army in France: 1917-1919* (Boston,
1936), pp. 56-7.

27.   Bliss' comment is appended to Joseph E. Kuhn to Chief of Staff, 28 May
1917. WCD 10050-34 in W.D. Historical File 7-31. RG 165 NA. The
estimate as to the length of time is in Kuhn to Chief of Staff, 7 June 1917,
WCD 10050-30 in War College Division File, RG 165 NA.

28.   Baker and Peyton C. March, 7 September 1927, Box 150. Newton D.
Baker Papers, Library of Congress. Also see previously cited Spector
article.

29.   Bliss to Pershing, 17 March 1921, Box 26, John J. Pershing Papers, Library
of Congress.

30.   Newton D. Baker, 'America in the World War', in Thomas G. Frothingham,
The American Reinforcement in the World War (Garden City, N.Y., 1927),
p. xxiii. Baker to Wilson, 8 May and Wilson to Baker, 10 May 1917, Box 4,
Baker Papers.

31.   John M. Palmer, 'Report of Board Considering Questions in the Zone of
the Army' file date 28 June 1917, Secret General Correspondence, AEF-
GHQ-6-3 no. 681, Part I, RG 120 NA. Hugh Drum who prepared this
report also served on the first committee. In his diary, 12-25 June, he
made several observations on the progress of the two committees' investi-
gations. Drum Papers.

32.   John J. Pershing, *My Experiences in the World War,* 2 vols. (New York,

1931), vol. I, pp. 80-86. The quotation is from page 80.

33.   *Ibid.,* vol. I, p. 293; Drum Diary, 7 September and 28 September to 14 October 1917.

34.   Fox Conner, LeRoy Eltinge, and Hugh Drum, 'A Strategical Study on the Employment of the A.E.F. Against the Imperial German Government', 25 September 1917, in AEF-GHQ-G-3 Secret General Correspondence no. 681, Part II, RG 120 NA.

35.   Pershing, *My Experiences,* vol. I, p. 213.

36.   James G. Harbord to Fox Conner, 1 January 1918, AEF-GHQ-6-3, Secret General Correspondence, no. 681, Part IV, RG 120 NA.

37.   Fox Conner to James G. Harbord, 7 January 1918, *ibid.*

38. This undated memo is attached to the two preceding documents.

39.   Maurice Hankey, *The Supreme Command,* 2 vols. (London, 1961), vol. II, pp. 764-5. See also Chapter LXXII on the manpower issue.

40.   Pershing,*My Experiences,* vol. I, pp. 309-10.

41.   Leonard P. Ayres, *The War with Germany: A Statistical Summary* (Washington, D.C., 1919), p. 37.

42.   Edward M. Coffman, *The War to End All Wars: The American Military Experience in World War I* (New York, 1968), pp. 171-2.

43.   Sir William Wiseman interview, 14 December 1960.

44.   Newton D. Baker to Tasker H. Bliss, 7 May 1918, Box 75, Bliss Papers.

45.   Ayres, *The War with Germany,* p. 37; Pershing, *My Experiences,* vol. I, p. 373.

46.   Diary, 31 May 1918, Box 1, Pershing Papers.

47.   Lloyd George quotation is from Hankey, op. cit., vol. II, p. 826. See Coffman, op. cit., pp. 285-298, 340.

48.   Major General George Van Horn Moseley interview, September 14, 1960. Moseley was the staff officer.

49.   William H. Carter to Pershing, 24 October 1918, Box 40, Pershing Papers.

50.   Major General Benjamin D. Foulois interview, 7 November 1960.

WAR AIMS AND STRATEGY: THE ITALIAN GOVERN-
MENT AND HIGH COMMAND 1914-1919

John Whittam

> To you, who have been born in Italy, God has allotted as if
> favouring you especially, the best defined country in Europe . . .
> God has stretched round you sublime and indisputable
> boundaries; on the one side the highest mountains of Europe,
> the Alps; on the other the sea, the immeasurable sea.

To Mazzini in 1869, that *annua mirabilis* of the Risorgimento, it all
seemed so simple. In the north, the arc of the Alps marked both the
natural and the national frontier of the Italian people and everywhere
else it was the sea. But, as Ettore Tolomei wrote some fifty-five years
later, frustrated by such imprecision, 'Which Alps, perdio!'[1] The acquisition of Lombardy and the loss of Savoy and Nice in 1859-60, had
produced viable borders with both France and Switzerland before the
creation of the new Kingdom of Italy in 1861.[2] The consequences of
the war with Austria in 1866 were less fortunate, because although
Ventia was redeemed and Italy reached up to the watershed in the
Carnic Alps, the Trentino and Alto Adige from the shores of Lake
Garda to the Brenner, the valley of the Isonzo in Venezia Giulia, Trieste
and Istria, all remained part of the Habsburg Monarchy. These areas
became *Italia Irredenta* for the next fifty years despite the fact that the
Alto Adige was predominantly German and the Isonzo and Istrian
regions were Slav. Between 1882 and 1915, when Italy was a partner of
Austria-Hungary through her membership of the Triple Alliance,
demands for the rectification of the north-eastern frontiers were naturally muted, but irredentists and strategically-minded soldiers were
determined to keep the issue alive. To his complaints about Mazzini's
vagueness over the Alpine frontiers, Tolomei could also have added,
'Which sea, perdio!' Apart from occasional calls for Italy to assert her
dominance over the entire Mediterranean, it was the Adriatic coastline
from Trieste to Valona which became something of an obsession for
those Italians who never tired of pointing out that there was no suitable naval base between Venice and Brindisi or that Dalmatia had been
part of the Venetian empire.

To these 'national aspirations' must be added Italy's imperial pre-

85

tensions which stemmed from her geographical position, her claim to great power status, and the virtually unavoidable decision to make Rome her capital. Significantly, it was anger at the French occupation of Tunisia which had led Italy to ally with Austria-Hungary and Germany in 1882 and thereby to renounce officially her claims to the unredeemed territories in the north. Temporarily thwarted in North Africa, she built up colonies in Eritrea and Somalia and sought, unsuccessfully, to penetrate the highlands of Ethiopia. In 1911-12, the war with Turkey led to the annexation of Libya and the occupation of the Dodecanese which, in turn, prompted Italy to extend her influence in the Balkans, Asia Minor and the Levant.

Italian aims, irredentist and imperialist, were well known before the outbreak of war in 1914. They placed an intolerable strain on the Triple Alliance because so many of the claims were at the expense of the Habsburg Monarchy and also caused embarrassment to the Entente Powers, particularly the Russians and the Americans. In addition, they posed acute problems for the Italian armed forces and for her diplomats. Perhaps most serious of all, they widened existing divisions within Italian society and created some new ones, wreaking such havoc that the old liberal state disintegrated in trying to cope with the post-war situation.

In May 1882, the international implications of Italian isolation appeared so alarming to the young deputy Sidney Sonnino that he wrote: 'the interests which we have in Trent are slight compared to those we have in establishing a sincere Friendship with Austria'.[3] Alberto Blanc, secretary-general at the foreign ministry, stressed the domestic perils and advocated an Austro-Italian agreement to safeguard the monarchy and the existing *status quo*.[4] The Italian Government, in its search for security, was specifically aiming at an alliance with Germany, but Bismarck had clearly indicated that the road to an understanding with Berlin lay through Vienna. Alliance with the hereditary enemy was unpalatable but unavoidable, and so the Triple Alliance was signed. Italy's traditional friendship with Britain was safeguarded by a ministerial declaration on 22 May 1882 which stipulated that the treaty was in no way directed against her. The preamble to the Triple Alliance emphasised the 'essentially conservative and defensive nature' of the agreement and there was no military convention, the nearest approach being article V which stated that if war appeared imminent 'the High Contracting Parties shall take counsel together in ample time as to the military measures to be taken with a view to eventual co-operation'.[5] In 1887, when the alliance was renewed Robilant, the Italian foreign minister, secured an amendment whereby the Austrians agreed that any change in the Balkans would necessitate prior consultations 'based upon the principle of reciprocal compensation'. At the same time, Germany agreed to protect Italian interests in North Africa.[6] In February 1888 a military convention was finally signed, Italy agreeing to send an expeditionary force to fight on the Rhine if the Triple Alliance went to war with France and Russia.[7] Membership of this power bloc undoubtedly had its advantages. The military, for instance, could largely ignore the threatening bulge of the Austrian Trentino and the Isonzo front, and concentrate on the French frontier which offered the Italians a strong defensive position. With a fleet which, for a time, ranked third in tonnage behind the British and French, and with the Mediterranean Agreements with Austria and Britain, Italy seemed at last secure on land and sea.[8] But there were disadvantages. The cost of maintaining a large army and navy in order to keep up with the military monarchies to the north was a crushing burden for a country poorly endowed with many of the basic raw materials, with an under-developed South, a high rate of illiteracy and constant financial problems.[9] Also, as the international situation grew more threatening after the conclusion of the Franco-Russian Alliance in 1894 and the beginnings of Anglo-German tension at the turn of the century, Italy's diplomatic position became more precarious. The possibility of her becoming involved in a major European war with Britain in the ranks of her enemies was so alarming that Italian diplomats hastened to assure all the Powers of her peaceful intentions and succeeded in making agreements with France, Britain and Russia. 'The Bible says', wrote an exasperated William II, 'no man can serve two masters, much less three! France, England and the Triplice.'[10] The appointment of Conrad von Hotzendorff as Austrian chief of staff in 1906 led to increasing tension between Italy and the Habsburg Monarchy. In 1908, Conrad argued that Austrian interests demanded 'the overthrow of Italy so as to rid ourselves in time of a probable enemy'.[11] Again, in 1911, when Italy was engaged in her war for Libya, he advocated a pre-emptive strike. General Pollio, the Italian chief of staff from 1908 to 1914 and a loyal supporter of the Triplice, felt that he could no longer ignore the threat to the north-eastern frontiers. The Bosnian crisis, the Agadir incident, the Libyan war and the Balkan wars which followed, all forced Italy to re-assess her international position.

Assisted by the international crises after 1908, Pollio and war minister Spingardi launched an ambitious programme of military reforms while the navy competed with Austria in the construction of dreadnoughts. Their plans were thrown into disarray by the Libyan war of 1911-12.[12] Giolitti and the military establishment had hoped for a *coup de théâtre* but the war proved long and costly. The military reform programme was disrupted and in November of 1912 Pollio sent Colonel Zupelli to Berlin to inform Moltke that Italy could no longer fulfil her commitments on the Rhine if war broke out. This did not prevent the fifth and final renewal of the Triple Alliance on 5 December 1912, nor the signing of the Triple Alliance Naval Convention in June 1913.[13] In September 1913 Pollio attended the German manoeuvres and reassured the Central Powers by announcing his willingness to send two cavalry divisions and three to five infantry divisions into south Germany via the Tyrol.[14] In February 1914 he informed his allies that Italian recovery had progressed sufficiently to allow the despatch of the Third Army to the Rhine as previously agreed. Outwardly at least, as Europe approached the July Crisis, Italy appeared to be more firmly attached to her Triple Alliance partners than ever before. But, as diplomats in every major capital realised, appearances could be deceptive.

As racial tension grew in the early years of the twentieth century, it became more and more difficult for the Italian Government and people to ignore the fate of nearly 800,000 Italians living under Habsburg rule. As evidence accumulated of the preferential treatment given by the authorities to Germans in the Trentino and Alto Adige, and to the Slovenes in Trieste, the old irredentist cries grew louder and demands for the 'rectification' of the frontier from the Brenner to Ragusa grew more insistent. With the growing popularity of D'Annunzio and Marinetti's Futurists, irredentism and nationalism began to merge. In the Alps and along the Adriatic, *italianita* was under threat from the rising tide of Pan-Germanism and Pan-Slavism. But for an exponent of *Realpolitik* like San Giuliano, Italian foreign minister from 1910 to October 1914, far more sinister were Austria's expanionist moves in the Balkans. This had led Italy to insist on the inclusion of the 'compensations' article when the Triple Alliance was renewed in 1912. Austria-Hungary and Italy in the famous article VII agreed that they would try to preserve the *status quo* in the Orient.

However, [the article continued] if, in the course of events, the

maintenance of the status quo in the regions of the Balkans or of the
Ottoman coasts and islands in the Adriatic and in the Aegean Sea
should become impossible and if ... Austria-Hungary and Italy should
find themselves under the necessity of modifying it by a temporary or
permanent occupation on their part, this occupation shall take place
only after a previous agreement between the two Powers, based upon
the principle of a reciprocal compensation for every advantage ... [15]

It was clearly understood that the compensation Italy had in mind was
the *terra irredenta*. It was also clearly understood that if the Central
Powers initiated hostilities in the Balkans or elsewhere no *casus foederis*
would arise compelling Italy to go to war.[16] Indeed, when friction arose
over the newly independent Albania and the Austrian demand for the
cession of Lovcen, San Giuliano declared his readiness to abandon his
allies and turn to the Entente.[17] But he soon realised that Italian aims
in the Balkans had raised the suspicions of Russia and that her preten-
sions in the Aegean and Adalia had irritated the French and British.
Italy was in danger of being on bad terms with all the Great Powers.
Nevertheless, San Giuliano continued to assert Italy's right to compensation if Austria disturbed the balance of power in the Balkans.[18]

   To an Italy shaken by the revolutionary events of Red Week, the
assassination of Franz Ferdinand on 28 June 1914 seemed relatively un-
important. The decision of Berlin and Vienna to use this as the pretext
for the humiliation of Serbia jolted Salandra's Government into a
sudden awareness that Italy now faced the tragic dilemma she had desperately hoped to avoid.

Although Pollio died just two days after the fatal assassination at Sarajevo,
his successor as chief of staff, Cadorna, confidently expected that Italy
would fulfil her obligations to the Central Powers if a European war
broke out. On 29 July, two days after he had assumed his new responsi-
bilities and one day after the outbreak of the Austro-Serbian war,
Cadorna asked the war minister to declare a state of readiness for all
units destined for the French frontier or the Rhine.[19] The Government's
decision to remain neutral, publicly announced on 2 August, took him by
surprise, and dismayed all those who were convinced of German invincibility. By 4 August all the Great Powers were at war. There was a universal
belief that the war would be short and, whichever side won, a neutral
and seemingly unprepared Italy faced a bleak future. The battle of the
Marne in early September and the onset of winter gave both Salandra and

Cadorna an opportunity to take stock of this perilous situation.

Unlike the Powers now locked in combat, Italy had formulated precise 'war aims' before firing a shot, indeed, before anyone had fired a shot. The term 'war aims' is perhaps inappropriate because the majority of Italians were opposed to war and the majority of politicians imagined that they could be achieved by peaceful means.[20] The German Government encouraged them in this belief and the Bülow mission to Rome from December 1914 to May 1915 was a prolonged attempt to keep Italy benevolently neutral by promising her compensation at the expense of the Habsburg Monarchy. The stubbornness of Vienna, the intrigues of the interventionist groups, and the military events in the first half of 1915, frustrated this attempt.[21]

This was as much a defeat for Giolitti and neutralist opinion in Italy as it was for German diplomacy. Although Giolitti had resigned the premiership in March 1914, his followers continued to dominate parliament and they remained solidly opposed to intervention until the Radiant May of 1915. Socialists and Catholics and the vast majority of the Italian people were also opposed to war as Sonnino, who became foreign minister in November 1914, admitted to Malagodi of the newspaper *Tribuna* on 12 December. Sonnino added, that if the Government decided upon war its duty was to ride roughshod over all those who stood in the way.[22] On 12 April 1915, Salandra sent out circulars to his prefects asking them to report on the public's attitude to the possibility of war. As he no doubt expected, the replies he received before he called off the survey on 21 April revealed an overwhelmingly neutralist sentiment. He was undismayed, however, as it was also apparent that the neutralists were hopelessly divided and politically apathetic.[23] Neither Salandra nor Sonnino were particularly impressed by the exploits of the interventionist groups which sprang up in the late autumn of 1914. Although they were to play an important role in May 1915, the noisy demonstrators who gathered around D'Annunzio, Marinetti and Mussolini endangered the delicate negotiations conducted by Sonnino and a tiny handful of collaborators from September 1914 to May 1915. They received bids from both the Central Powers and the Entente countries, but Salandra, Sonnino and Martini, the colonial minister, seem to have decided upon intervention against Austria-Hungary after a secret meeting on 17 September.[24]

The Italian supporters of the Triplice did not give in without a struggle. Sonnino himself, in early August, spoke of honouring the agreements made with the Central Powers.[25] Bollati, the ambassador in Berlin, was convinced of a German victory and Avarna in Vienna wrote that Italy, by

abandoning her allies, had 'lost sight of what should be one of our aims
– the command of the Mediterranean'. They also pointed out that if there
were kinsmen in Austria, there was also an *irredenta* in Corsica, Nice, and
Malta.[26] But after the battle of the Marne such arguments were seldom
heard. Much more common was the thesis which earned Giolitto so much
unjustified notoriety in February 1915. In his so-called *parecchio* letter,
Giolitti remarked that Italy could gain 'quite a lot' by simply remaining
neutral. As Seton-Watson has pointed out: 'By publishing it, Giolitti unin-
tentionally assumed the leadership of all the neutralist forces and turned
the campaign for intervention into an anti-Giolitti crusade.'[27]

Advocates of intervention on the side of the Entente could produce
a much more impressive list of war aims than the supporters of the
Triple Alliance or those with a *parecchio* mentality. The Trentino and
Alto Adige, the Isonzo frontier, Trieste, Istria and the Dalmatian coast
could all be claimed from Austria-Hungary and be allotted to Italy in
the event of an Entente victory. Albania, which Italy had begun to
occupy in December 1914, would become an Italian satellite and con-
vert the Adriatic into an Italian lake. The decision of the Turks to join
the Central Powers led Italy to expect an even larger share of the
Ottoman Empire than she had envisaged before 1914. The pro-German
stance of the Greek king would assist Italian efforts to retain the
Dodecanese and preserve southern Albania from Greek claims. In
Africa, Anglo-French support would enable Italy to extend her colonial
possessions. In addition, the wealth of the Entente might be expected to
help finance the war and Welsh coal would provide fuel for the fleet. It
was, of course, easier to draw up this shopping list than to secure its
implementation. As the British foreign secretary Grey had written, 'in
war words count only so far as they are backed by force and
victories'.[28] Because they were war aims they naturally involved Italy in
war, certainly with Austria and probably also with Germany. Italy had
no outstanding disagreements with the Reich, and for over forty years
Italians had admired German achievements and respected her military
and economic strength.[29] Salandra hoped to fight a limited war, a
piccolo guerra directed solely against the Austrians to complete the
unfinished business of the Risorgimento.[30] Italy went to war with
Austria-Hungary in May 1915 and with Germany only in August 1916,
so to this extent Salandra was successful. Apart from compelling Italy
to fight one or possibly two Great Powers, these war aims had to be
sold to the Entente countries.

As Serbian and Italian war aims were in conflict along the

Adriatic, it was surprising that Russia made the initial moves to win over Italy to the side of the Entente. In August and September 1914, Sasonov, the Russian foreign minister, was prepared to sacrifice Slav interests in the Balkans if Italy immediately attacked the Austrians.[31] Italy felt unable to commit herself and Russian interest began to wane. In any case, on 4 September 1914 the three Entente Powers had signed a treaty which pledged them to co-ordinate their diplomacy until a satisfactory peace was secured. The Italians were keen to prolong negotiations and to transfer them from Petrograd to London. Grey was agreeable but steadfastly refused to act behind the backs of his allies or to consider mere hypotheses as the basis for firm diplomatic commitments. Between October and March 1915 the Allies showed no sense of urgency in their dealings with Italy and Russia became distinctly cool. The Rome Government during the winter months became preoccupied with meeting the German diplomatic offensive headed by Bülow and keeping the Austrians in play. The Italians had occupied Valona in December 1914 and Sonnino made it plain that he had no intention of allowing Albania to become a substitute for *Italia irredenta*.[32] Despite German pressure, Austria stubbornly resisted efforts to make her agree to the surrender of Habsburg territory and this enabled Rome to spin out negotiations with the Central Powers while she came to terms with the Entente and prepared the army for war. The turning point came in early March. On 3 March Salandra instructed his ambassador in London, Imperiali, to hand over the Italian proposals which had been held in readiness for some months, and on 9 March the Austrians finally succumbed and agreed to consider the question of compensations.[33] On the military front, the Russian advance in Galicia and the Allied attack on the Dardanelles, seemed to herald the collapse of the Habsburg and Ottoman empires. Italian intervention, which might also induce the Rumanians, Greeks and Bulgarians to enter the war, might well deliver the *coup de grace*. The Entente, for the first time since September, believed that Italian cooperation would be the turning point of the war. The British and French were even willing to promise Constantinople to the Russians in order to secure it. On the Italian side it was realised that if they missed this opportunity to intervene and the Entente won the war without their assistance, their claims and their very status as a Great Power would be in jeopardy. To extricate Italy from the negotiations with Vienna, Sonnino sent, on 8 April, a series of unacceptable terms to Burian, the new Austrian foreign minister, terms which even the Italian ambassador described as conditions which a victor might

impose upon a completely prostrate enemy.[34] Negotiations with the
Entente were speeded up and the Treaty of London was signed on 26
April. In return for denouncing the Triple Alliance and going to war
with Austria-Hungary, which she did on 4 May and 24 May respectively,
Italy was promised the Brenner frontier, Trieste and Istria, the line of
the Julian Alps, central Dalmatia and its islands, Valona and its hinter-
land, and the Dodecanese.[35] Fiume and the southern Dalmatian coastline would, suitably demilitarised, be available to the Croats and Serbs.
This secret treaty, which was to create so much dissension in the years
to come, was almost destroyed by events in the middle of May. The
Russian defeat at Gorlice and the Allied failure to force the Straits
lowered the prestige of the Entente, and on 9 May Giolitti returned to
Rome to rally his followers and, perhaps, to take advantage of last
minute efforts by Bülow and Erzberger to draw up a satisfactory
Italo-Austrian compromise. Salandra's resignation on 13 May seemed a
triumph for neutralism but Giolitti rejected the offer of the premiership and on the 16th Salandra resumed the reins of the Government.
Giolitti's withdrawal disheartened his three hundred or so supporters in
the chamber and interventionist mobs created the illusion that Italian
opinion overwhelmingly favoured intervention. On 20 May when parliament reassembled it voted full powers for the Salandra Government and
four days later Italy went to war. The diplomats had achieved their
renversement des alliances and a small conspiratorial group around
Salandra had completed a most remarkable *tour de force.* It now remained for the army to implement the war aims of the Treaty of
London.

To be in a position to launch an offensive war against Austria had also
involved great skill and tenacity. In early August 1914, Cadorna and
the general staff were prepared for a defensive war in the French Alps
while a large Italian contingent assisted in a German blitzkrieg in
northern France. Italy's declaration of neutrality forced Cadorna to revise all existing war plans. Men and materials had to be transferred to
the north-eastern frontiers where the Trentino salient and the Isonzo
front, both legacies of that inglorious war of 1866, presented Cadorna
with tactical and strategic nightmares. Along this 484-mile frontier
there were three distinct sectors: the Trentino, where Cadorna decided
to remain on the defensive, the Carnic Alps and Dolomites where alti-
tude and terrain prevented large-scale operations, and the Isonzo front.
It was only in this last sector that a decisive breakthrough seemed feas-

ible, although it was argued that 'the river could not be crossed until the mountains had been seized, and the mountains could not be seized until the river had been crossed'.[36] Between June 1915 and September 1917, Cadorna launched eleven assaults in this area but failed to achieve a breakthrough. Unlike Salandra, Cadorna did not believe that Italy could fight her own *piccolo guerra,* remaining aloof from the *grande guerra* being waged by the other belligerents. At first, he was convinced that Italy's entry into the war, after the winter months of 1914-15 had allowed her time to reorganise and re-equip, would be decisive and brief. In the senate in April 1915 he had explained to his questioners that within a month he would be in Trieste and menacing the heart of the Habsburg Empire.[37] Hopefully, the Italian troops would link up with the advancing Russians, Serbs and Rumanians — and perhaps also an Allied army moving up from Salonika — roll up the Eastern Front and end the war. Such aims were always too grandiose for Salandra and Sonnino; the premier, because he realised that such a war required total mobilisation of the country's resources which could well dislocate the *status quo* within the country; the foreign minister, because he was appalled at the prospect of the complete disintegration of the Habsburg Monarchy as this would enable the Russians and their Slav allies to sweep down to the shores of the Adriatic. When Cadorna attacked in June 1915, his allies had stopped advancing and Sonnino's diplomacy had failed to bring in the Rumanians. Alone, Italy could only make limited gains against the well-entrenched defensive positions of the Austrians. Like all the other commanders in the war, Cadorna was committed to frontal attacks and a war of attrition.[38] Fighting in the wasteland of the Isonzo or the Carso, ignorant of the existence of Trieste or Trento, the majority of the troops failed to see why they were suffering such frightful losses for such worthless territory. Their basic war aims were survival and a train ticket back home.[39]

A surprise Austrian attack from the Trentino in May 1916 brought to a head the conflict between Salandra and Cadorna which had smouldered on for almost a year. This *Stafexpedition,* which Cadorna managed to contain, brought down Salandra and discredited his concept of the war.[40] His successor Boselli declared war on Germany in August 1916 and Italy moved perceptively closer to total involvement in the *grande guerra.* Cadorna had survived the May crisis, but although he sought closer links with his allies and regarded the Italian contribution as part of the overall strategy of the Entente, he could never fully adapt himself to the demands, physical and psychological, of total war. Sonnino also survived, stubbornly resolved to cling to the original war aims despite increasing opposition among the Allies and within Italy itself.

Italian claims in the Balkans and Sonnino's obsessive concern for the Adriatic led Albertini to describe the Treaty of London as 'a serious obstacle to the success of our arms'.[41] Slavs both inside and outside the Habsburg Monarchy regarded Italy with increasing distrust and this undoubtedly hampered the Allied war effort and raised serious questions concerning any post-war settlement. Sonnino's preoccupation with Dalmatia and the Slav menace had also caused him to pay scant attention to Italy's wider aims in the Mediterranean and in Africa. The Treaty of London noted Italy's interest 'in the maintenance of the balance of power in the Mediterranean', it had promised a 'just share' in the Adalia region if Turkey were partitioned, and in Africa she was promised 'equitable compensation'. But this was all terribly vague compared to the precise enumeration of Dalmatian islands in other clauses. If Italy hoped to put forward colonial claims at a future peace conference or assert her influence beyond the Adriatic the treaty of 1915 was scarcely a firm foundation. Equally lax had been Sonnino's treatment of economic and financial consideratins. Had the war been short, this would have been overlooked, but as it dragged on and on Italian resources became dangerously depleted. But it was events in 1917 which made the Treaty of London appear increasingly anachronistic.

The Russian revolution, the entry of the USA into the war, the consequences of the battle of Caporetto, and the accumulation of evidence pointing to the dissolution of the Habsburg Monarchy, all had their impact on Italian war aims and propaganda. Even before any of these momentous events had taken place, however, disagreement over war aims had become apparent among the Allies. After months of persistent enquiries Sonnino had at last been informed, towards the end of 1916, of the Anglo-French offer of Constantinople to Russia and of the Sykes-Picot agreement of February 1916. Alarmed, and belatedly interested in the fate of the Ottoman Empire, Sonnino strove to safeguard Italy's position in this area. He achieved some successes but in the process irritated all his allies and alienated the Venizelos faction in Greece.[42] A compromise of St Jean de Maurienne in April 1917 papered over the cracks.[43] News of these negotiations leaked out and helped to provoke furious debates about war aims among Italians themselves. Meanwhile in revolutionary Petrograd, demands were made for the revision of war aims in the interests of a peace 'without annexations or indemnities'. Similar statements came from Washington where President Wilson also called for a 'new diplomacy', a democratic crusade against militarism and imperialism, and a just peace based on national self-determination. These were sentiments which were echoed by men like Bissolati in Italy but were contemptuously dismissed both by Sonnino, still the upholder of Salandra's narrow *sacro egoismo,* and by the nationalists and imperialists who now put forward expansionist claims far in excess of those agreed in the Treaty of London. The defeat at Carporetto and Italy's closer integration with the Allied war effort only constituted a truce in this furious war aims debate which continued on into 1918, 1919 and beyond.

Caporetto and the Italian retreat to the Piave had led to the formation of a government under Orlando and the replacement of Cadorna by Diaz. But Sonnino remained foreign minister and, as Bissolati complained, he steadfastly refused to acknowledge that the situation had been completely transformed. Building ramparts in the Adriatic against imperial Russia had become nonsensical since the revolution. The Slavs no longer looked to Petrograd and if Italy renounced her extensive claims to Dalmatia she could become the natural ally of all the subject peoples of the foundering Habsburg Monarchy, which had been one of Mazzini's noblest aspirations. Bissolati was also unhappy about Italian annexationism in the Tyrol, fearing that Italy might inherit the unenviable role of the nearly defunct Austrian Empire.[44]

Neither the proclamation of Wilson's Fourteen Points on 8 January 1918 — clearly incompatible with the Treaty of London — nor deputy Bevione's public reading of that treaty on 13 February shook Sonnino's determination to resist all attempts to revise Italian war aims, nor did the close military and economic collaboration with the Allies after Caporetto induce him to be more accommodating. Nevertheless, on 8 April 1918 a Congress of Oppressed Nationalities gathered at Rome. It was an impressive gathering. The Italian delegates included Albertini, Barzilai, Mussolini, Amendola, Martini, Federzoni, Prezzolini and Savemini representing all factions from the irredentists and nationalists to democrats and republicans.[45] With the apparent blessing of Orlando but not, of course, of Sonnino, they mingled with Czechs, Slovaks, Rumanians and Jugoslavs and produced the *Patto di Roma* as a kind of counter-blast to the *Patto di Londra.* All the nationalities present, including delegates from France and Wickham Steed for Britain, pledged themselves to unconditional solidarity in the struggle for the redemption of oppressed peoples, and Italians and Jugoslavs recognised their mutual interest in the national self-determination of their respective countries.[46] They resolved to settle all frontier disputes in a spirit of fraternity that reminded many of them — and also Orlando — of the prophecies of Mazzini. Although the Pact helped to remove much of the bitterness created by the publication of the Treaty of London and assisted a hard-pressed Italy by winning over many of the subject nationalities within the Habsburg Monarchy, Sonnino remained unconvinced and unrepentant, refusing to recognise the official validity of the Pact of Rome. Even after Italy aligned herself with the other Entente countries in recognising the Czech state, thereby dooming the Habsburg Empire, Sonnino refused to acknowledge the feasibility of any Jugoslav state.

Throughout, the failure of the army and navy to achieve any strategic successes deprived Sonnino of that leverage conferred by military victory and the occupation of enemy territory. Eleven times Cadorna had battered away on the Izonzo front, seeking to break through to Trieste and head for the Ljubljana gap.[47] Apart from the capture of Gorizia in the summer of 1916, Italian gains had been incommensurate with the appalling losses. Cadorna, unlike Salandra or Sonnino, had always viewed the Italian contribution as part of the overall grand strategy of the Entente. He had opposed colonial and Albanian diversions but was prepared to assist his allies in Salonika and on the Western Front. He had, however, in the early autumn of 1917 failed to press energetically enough for an Allied offensive on the Italian front which, until the Nivelle mirage began to flicker, had attracted the support of Lloyd George and all those who sought to break the western stalemate by some flanking movement. The Austro-German attack, which an Allied build-up on the Isonzo would have forestalled, finally took place on 24 October 1917. Although long awaited, it achieved a tactical and strategic surprise. The battle of Caporetto threw the Italians back to the Piave, just short of Venice. This advance into Italian territory convinced many Italians that they must modify their war aims, but there were perhaps even more on whom it had the reverse effect. Mussolini, for instance, exclaiming that before Caporetto he had been content with the terms of the Treaty of London, but that afterwards he demanded the whole of Dalmatia. Diaz, the new commander, held the line of the Piave, beating off Austrian attempts to smash through. Only on 24 October 1918 did Diaz feel confident enough to throw his 57 divisions, including 3 British and 2 French, into a final offensive. In this

battle of Vittorio Veneto, the Austrian collapse began on 29 October.
On 3 November Udine and Trent were occupied and an armistice
signed at the Villa Giusti. Hostilities ceased, but the Italian advance did
not. These were the days in which the Italian army and fleet at last ful-
filled the expectations of Sonnino and took over the territories promised by the Treaty of London. For the first time, now the war was
over, war aims and military conquest roughly coincided.

The Austro-Hungarian collapse produced a vacuum on the north-
eastern frontiers and along the Adriatic which the Italians were determined to fill. They could not afford to be dilatory or too courteous
with their allies. On 29 October, the day of the Austrian army's final
disintegration, the Narodno Vijece proclaimed the independence of the
Serbs, Croats and Slovenes amidst scenes of jubiliation in Zagreb. News
of this, together with well-founded rumours that Emperor Charles was
handing over the Austro-Hungarian fleet to the Slavs, produced conster-
nation in Rome.[48] Just as Italy reached out for the rewards of victory,
the Jugoslavs were preparing to snatch them away. Italy had lost over
700,000 killed and one million wounded and spent over 400 milliards.[49]
Sonnino was not alone in feeling that this was too high a price for
making the world safe for a disorganised rabble calling themselves Jugoslavs.

On 31 October 1918 the Supreme War Council at Versailles approved
the terms of the impending armistices with the Central Powers. The
demarcation line in the Balkans 'corresponded in almost every detail to
the 1915 Treaty of London line'.[50] As the Austrians withdrew, Allied
forces were expected to move in but, owing to Italy's proximity and
eagerness, Italian troops and sailors were certain to arrive first and act
as the representative of all the Allies. The Allies ordered the Jugoslavs
to sail the Austro-Hungarian fleet, which had mutinied at Pola on the
29th, to Corfu but in the event it was divided up between the Italians
and the Jugoslavs. Very swiftly, Italian units moved up to and beyond
the demarcation line. Allied forces arrived in early November but were
small in size and placed under the command of Diaz. Fiume, which
had not been allocated to Italy, was occupied by a Serbian battalion on
18 November but the Italians tricked them into withdrawing and then
occupied the city themselves. Within a few days of the armistice,
Italian arrogance had alienated everyone including the British and
French. Nevertheless, neither the Jugoslavs nor the Allies wished to
provoke Italy into major hostilities so, at the cost of total isolation,
Italy — to the despair of men like Bissolati — was allowed to pursue her

disastrous course. It was Orlando who personally authorised the seizure of Fiume, so Bissolati's belief that the premier would restrain Sonnino was unfounded.[51] The lengths to which both the civilian and military leaders were prepared to go in their peace-time campaign is revealed in a letter by Badoglio which won the support of Diaz, Orlando and Sonnino. In it he outlined a scheme for setting up a network of agents in Jugoslav territory with orders to use the religious, regional and political divisions among the Slavs to disrupt the unity which they had had the temerity to proclaim on 1 December 1918. It was scarcely surprising that Bissolati, who advocated the renunciation of Dalmatia in order to secure Fiume, resigned that month from a cabinet which seemed determined to press for the full implementation of the Treaty of London and for the incorporation of Fiume and other areas not mentioned in that document.[52]

The successes and failures of the Italian delegation at the Paris Peace Conference need not be retold in any detail, nor can the disruptive issue of Fiume between 1919 and 1924 be pursued in this study.[53] Italian intransigence before the official opening of the conference on 18 January 1919 had already irritated the Americans, who were not bound by the Treaty of London, and the British and French, who were. When Italo-Jugoslav claims were first discussed before the Council of Ten on 18 February Sonnino was as inflexible as ever, rejecting Balfour's suggestion that they should be referred to an expert commission and he refused to acknowledge any decision which had not been negotiated in the Supreme Council itself.[54] Sonnino also protested violently when it was decided to tackle the German problem first, becoming more and more irritated and irritating by the failure of the conference to discuss Italian affairs. By April, when the Council of Four finally confronted the Italian problem, nationalist passions on both sides of the Adriatic were running high. The Italian ambassador in Paris informed Balfour that the surrender of Fiume would bring down the Italian Government, perhaps provoke an army revolt and 'probably produce a violent explosion of indignation in that country'.[55] On 19 April, when Orlando presented the Italian case, there was certainly an explosion in the Council of Four. He demanded the Brenner frontier and Dalmatia on strategic grounds, despite the fact that Diaz regarded the latter as militarily untenable,[56] and Fiume on the basis of national self-determination. Since January, Wilson had accepted the Brenner frontier, despite the quarter of a million German inhabitants, and perhaps because of

this breach in his principles he was particularly responsive to the Jugoslavs who had turned to him as mediator in February. Wilson opposed
the Treaty of London line in Dalmatia and supported the partition of
Istria on national grounds, but rejected Italian claims to Fiume because
it had not been included in the treaty of 1915 and was an essential
outlet for the new successor states. Everyone participating in this acri-
monious discussion became aware of their own inconsistencies and this
increased the bitterness. Total breakdown occurred on 23 April when
Wilson published a manifesto to the Italian people and Orlando walked
out of the conference. The President's action achieved the remarkable
result of temporarily uniting all Italians, not behind Wilson's programme of moderation but against it. Rapturously acclaimed by the
Italian people, Orlando repudiated the compromise solution of making
Fiume a free city and glorified Italy's stand against the rest of the
world. 'Never have I felt so proud to be an Italian', exclaimed
D'Annunzio, whose exaltation was shared by the entire nation. Meanwhile, the Council of Three went about its business, allotting mandates
to Britain and France, inviting the Greeks to land in Smyrna, and, in
general ignoring Italy's claims in Africa and the Ottoman Empire. In
addition, Lloyd George threatened that if the Italians refused to return
to Paris, the Allies would sign peace with Germany, leave Italy to make
her own arrangements and regard the Treaty of London as null and
void,[57] Sonnino and Orlando returned and took their seats again on
7 May. They were prepared to make some concessions in the
Adriatic — and to replace British troops in the Caucasus[58] — but
Wilson was still dissatisfied and no compromise was reached. On 19
June, nine days before all the Allies signed the treaty with Germany,
the Orlando Government fell. Sonnino, still acting as plenipotentiary,
signed the peace treaty with Germany at Versailles on 28 June. It was
perhaps appropriate that he was not asked to sign the Treaty of St
Germain with Austria on 10 September.[59]

Alone amongst the belligerents, Italy had entered the First World War
with a precise list of war aims enshrined in the Treaty of London. Apart
from the fateful addition of Fiume, these were what the Italian representatives sought to implement in 1919. The real reason why the Italian
Government went to war in 1915, as Salandra admitted, was to prove
her Great Power status. Abstention from that conflict would have revealed Italy's unwillingness or unpreparedness to confirm this status.
The stalemate along the Italo-Austrian front, Rome's apparent reluc-

tance to enter wholeheartedly into the *grande guerra* and the defeat at Caporetto, did not provide this confirmation. Her exaltation in the final weeks of the war, her frenetic activities after the armistice, and the stubborn persistence of Orlando and Salandra during the peace negotiations can therefore be easily understood, even if they appear misconceived. They were all part of a last, desperate attempt to show the world — and the Italian people — that Italy had qualified as a Great Power. Fiume, a not very spectacular Adriatic port, became the touchstone of greatness. It is not without significance, that only two days after St Germain D'Annunzio's legionaries occupied the city. Italian sensitivity during and after the war had serious repercussions. A constant fear of being slighted led to an arrogance on the part of many military and civilian leaders which alienated Italy's allies, alarmed her neighbours in the Balkans, and so increased the volatility of Italian public opinion that the very existence of the old liberal state was threatened.

The final irony is that Italy, despite the widespread belief in a 'multilated victory', had achieved a great deal. The possession of Trent and Trieste was the realisation of an age-old dream. The strategic strength of the Brenner frontier outweighed the disadvantages of incorporating a quarter of a million Germans. Around Tarvisio, Italy annexed Slovene territory that had not been included in the Treaty of London. Despite the lack of interest shown by her negotiators, Italy received a share of German reparations and a permanent seat on the Council of the new League of Nations. Britain and France were prepared to listen to Italian demands in Africa, and although they were unlikely to acquiesce in the cession of Djibouti or the granting of a mandate in Togoland, frontier rectifications of existing Italian colonies and a protectorate in Ethiopia were distinct possibilities. Possession of the Dodecanese and interests in Adalia kept open the door to future Italian expansion in that area until it was firmly shut by Kemal. On 2 August 1920, Giolitti and Sforza withdrew troops from Albania, except for the island of Saseno, and relinquished their claim to a mandate.[60] This generosity impressed the Allies and when the Italians met the Jugoslavs at Rapallo in November 1920 Sforza was assured of Great Power support for his claims. By the treaty signed on 12 November, Italy gained the Monte Nevosa line in Istria — in effect the Treaty of London line rather than that drawn by Wilson — Fiume became a free state in contiguity with Italy, and its annexation by Mussolini in 1924 was something of a formality. Italy also won the islands of Cres, Losinj,

Palagruza and Lastovo and sovereignty over Zara. Together with Pola in the north, this satisfied the claims of the navy without placing an excessive defence burden on the army.[61]

Unfortunately, the bitter inter-Allied conflict in 1919, constant clashes with the Jugoslavs, and the Fiume episode had all contributed to a mood of angry frustration. The majority of Italians viewed the Versailles settlement, the League of Nations, and their war-time allies with a cynicism and contempt which played into the hands of a fascist movement eager to use this disillusionment for the conquest of power. In this respect, the war aims and the manner of their implementation served the interests of Mussolini rather than Italy.

Notes

1. D. Rusinow, *Italy's Austrian Heritage 1919-46* (Oxford, 1969), pp. 16-18. Tolomei and his propagandist collaborators were also guilty of vague statements such as: 'Polybius, one of the most famous historians of the Roman epoch, clearly states that as far back as the year 241 before Christ the name Italia was used to designate all the lands extending from the Alps to Sicily' (M. Alberti, E. Tolomei *et al., Italy's Great War and her National Aspirations* (Milan, 1917), p. 68).
2. Nice, Savoy and the Ticino were, of course, claimed by exalted nationalists from time to time.
3. G. Volpe, *L'Italia nella triplice alleanza* (Milan, 1941), pp. 30-3.
4. L. Salvatorelli, *La triplice alleanza* (Milan, 1939), p. 61.
5. A. Pribram, *The Secret Treaties of Austria-Hungary 1879-1915* (Harvard, 1920), vol. I, pp. 65-9.
6. *Ibid.*, pp. 109, 113.
7. *Documenti diplomatici italiani,* 2nd series, XXI, p. 520.
8. For the best recent discussion on the naval situation see P. Halpern, *The Mediterranean Naval Situation 1908-1914* (Harvard, 1971).
9. L. De Rosa, 'Incidenza delle spese militari sullo sviluppo economico italiano', *Atti del primo convegno nazionale di storia militare* (Rome, 1969), pp. 183-219.
10. L. Albertini, *The Origins of the War of 1914* (Oxford, 1952), vol. I, p. 175.
11. *Ibid.,* p. 194.
12. J. Whittam, *The Politics of the Italian Army 1861-1918* (London, 1976), pp. 165-9.
13. Halpern, *Mediterranean Naval Situation,* pp. 220-52.
14. Earlier plans to send Italian troops through neutral Switzerland are discussed in M. Mazzetti, 'L'Italia e le convenzioni militari secrete della Triplice Alleanza', *Storia contemporanes,* I (June, 1970).
15. Z. Zeman, *A Diplomatic History of the First World War* (London, 1971), p. 3.
16. It was this argument which convinced the cabinet of 31 July 1914 that an Italian declaration of neutrality was justified (F. Martini, *Il Diario 1914-18* (Milan, 1966), p. 7).

17. *Origins of the War,* vol. I, pp. 518-19.
18. *DDI,* 4th series, XII, p. 225.
19. G. Rochat, 'L'esercito italiano nell'estate del 1914', *Nuova rivista storica,* 45, 1961, 324, f. 2.
20. A. Monticone, 'Sonnino e Salandra verso la decisione dell 'intervento', *Gli italiani in uniforme* (Bari, 1972), pp. 57-87.
21. The most detailed account of German policies is A. Monticone, *La Germania e la neutralita italiana* (Bologna, 1971).
22. O. Malagodi, *Conversazioni della guerra* (Milan, 1960), vol. I, p. 32.
23. B. Vigezzi, *Da Diolitti a Salandra* (Florence, 1969), pp. 321-402.
24. Martini, *Il Diario,* p. 103.
25. S. Sonnino, *Diario 1914-1916* (Bari, 1972), vol. II, p. 12.
26. W. Gottlieb, *Studies in Secret Diplomacy* (London, 1957), pp. 150-2.
27. C. Seton-Watson, *Italy from Liberalism to Fascism* (London, 1967), p. 439.
28. Grey of Fallodon, *Twenty-five Years* (London, 1928), vol. II, p. 106.
29. A classic treatment of this is in F. Chabod, *Storia della politica estera italiana dal 1870 al 1896,* vol. I, *Le premesse* (Bari, 1951).
30. See A. Salandra, *La neutralita italiana* (Milan, 1928); and also his *L'Intervento (1915). Ricordi e pensieri* (Milan, 1930). For a brief discussion see J. Whittam, 'War and Italian Society 1914-6', in B. Bond and I. Roy (eds.), *War and Society* (London, 1975).
31. C. Lowe, 'Britain and Italian Intervention 1914-15', *The Historical Journal,* vol. XII, no. 3 (1969), p. 534.
32. Sonnino, *Diario,* vol. II, p. 70.
33. Salandra, *L'Intervento,* p. 149.
34. In return for her continued neutrality, Italy demanded the cession of the Trentino, the frontier districts around Gradisca and Gorizia, and the Curzola archipelago; Trieste was to be established as an independent state and Albania recognised as an Italian sphere. The ceded territories were to be occupied immediately (Gottlieb, *Studies in Secret Diplomacy,* pp. 365-6).
35. The text can be found in R. Albrecht-Carrié, *Italy at the Paris Peace Conference* (New York, 1938), pp. 334-9.
36. P. Pieri, 'The Italian Front', in V. Esposito (ed.), *A Concise History of World War I* (London, 1965), pp. 161-2.
37. F. Nitti, *Rivelazioni, Dramatis personae* (Naples, 1948), pp. 183-4.
38. P. Pieri, *L'Italia nella prima guerra mondiale* (Turin, 1965), pp. 65-6.
39. P. Melograni, *Storia politica della grande guerra* (Bari, 1969), p. 13. See also the moving accounts in A. Omodeo, *Momenti della vita di guerra,* new ed. (Turin 1968).
40. J. Whittam, 'War and Italian Society 1914-16', p. 158.
41. L. Albertini, *Venti anni di vita politica* (Bologna, 1953), vol. IV, p. 10.
42. Seton-Watson, *Italy from Liberalism,* p. 463.
43. M. Toscano, *Gli accordi di San Giovanni di Moriana* (Milan, 1936), pp. 340-2.
44. Malagodi, *Conversazioni della Guerra,* vol. II, pp. 263-4.
45. *Ibid.,* II, pp. 322-3. Martini, *Il Diario,* pp. 1126-7.
46. Albrecht-Carrié, *Italy at the Paris Conference,*pp. 347-8.
47. E. Faldella, *La grande guerra. Le battaglie dell'Isonzo 1915-17* (Milan, 1965), vol. I, pp. 36-7.
48. I. Lederer, *Yugoslavia at the Paris Peace Conference* (Yale, 1963), p. 43.
49. Ufficio storico, *L'Esercito Italiano* (Rome, 1961), p. 227.
50. Lederer, *Yugoslavia at the Paris Peace Conference,* p. 54. For the Italian

moves in Dalmatia and Fiume see pp. 56-78.

51.   *Ibid.,* p. 63. Malagodi, *Conversazione della Guerra,* vol. II, p. 438.

52.   The plan was submitted on 3 December 1918 and approved by Sonnino on the 9th (Lederer, *Yugoslavia,* pp. 71-5).

53.   Albrecht-Carrié and Lederer give full accounts. Consult also, A. Mayer, *Politics and Diplomacy of Peacemaking* (London, 1969) and H. Elcock, *Portrait of a Decision* (London, 1972).

54.   Elcock, *Portrait of a Decision,* p. 116.

55.   *Ibid.,* p. 220.

56.   When questioned, Diaz had explained that the Adriatic was an obsession of Thaon de Revel and the naval authorities, that to secure the defence of the islands and the adjacent coast would require a military presence which would be a constant source of weakness for Italy (Malagodi, *Conversazioni della Guerra,* vol. II, pp. 503-4).

57.   D. Lloyd George, *The Truth about the Peace Treaties* (London, 1930), vol. II, pp. 868-9.

58.   Sonnino, *Diario 1916-22,* vol. III, pp. 338-40.

59.   Uncharacteristically, he supported swift ratification of both treaties. They were, in fact, ratified on 10 January 1920 and 16 July 1920 (*ibid.,* vol. III, p. 347).

60.   Lederer, *Yugoslavia,* pp. 290-1.

61.   *Ibid.,* p. 305.

GERMAN WAR AIMS 1914-1918 AND GERMAN POLICY BEFORE THE WAR

Fritz Fischer

With the theme of my paper, I am faced with the question of whether there is a definite connection between German war aims 1914-18 and German policy before the war — in other words, whether it is correct to speak of continuity. To begin my examination I wish to look back somewhat.

The German Reich came into existence through the diplomacy of Bismarck and as a result of three short wars which he had 'willed and waged' (*gewollt und gemacht*, to quote Bethmann Hollweg, his successor fourth in line). In that Reich, the State of Prussia prevailed with its special characteristics: particularly the dominance of the military and the bureaucracy, and within them both of the East Elbian Junker class — whereas the middle class, the 'bourgeoisie', represented in the 'Reichstag' and in the federal 'Landtage' at no time reached a political position really corresponding to its economic importance. Originally and essentially an agrarian state, Germany rapidly developed around the turn of the century into the second commercial power after Great Britain and into the second industrial power after the USA. This development was accompanied by an enhanced welfare and rashly overweening self-confidence, but nonetheless overshadowed by the mushrooming growth of an industrial labour force, organised for the most part in Social Democracy, which Bismarck in vain attempted both to hold at bay by means of exceptional laws and at the same time to win over by means of a seductive social policy. From the 1890s onwards this work force weighed like a nightmare on the feudal and bourgeois world. The earlier conflict between the agrarian and industrial interests, directed on the one side against Russia and on the other against England and the USA, had been bridged over by Bismarck's protectionist policy — a constellation which lasted, in spite of many frictions, until World War I.

In the realm of foreign relations the German Reich under Bismarck, by virtue of his alliance policy, occupied a 'semi-hegemonial' (Dehio)[1] position in Europe, one which was acknowledged by Britain, regarding her tensions with Russia and France, but which was impaired by the conclusion of the Russo-French Defensive Alliance of 1894, precipitated by Bismarck's own policy and that of his successor Caprivi. Thereafter a war situation necessarily entailed for Germany the very real danger of a two-front war. While Caprivi's commercial treaty policy sought to broaden the central European basis of the Reich, economic expansion pressed in the direction of overseas territories. Industrial development took place within a framework of enduring and increasingly trouble-some scarcity of capital and in the face of competitive pressure from the USA, Japan, Britain and France. Of these powers the last two had the advantage of superior capital resources.

'Weltpolitik' and Navalism

Such was the background to the transition to *weltpolitik* and navalism. Whatever the precise distribution of emphasis in the motivation under-lying German policy — whether it was pre-eminently or exclusively domestic political motives, as H.U. Wehler and V.R. Berghahn main-tain,[2] who view the navy as an instrument for rallying the nation against Social Democracy (social imperialism in other words); whether it was the economic interests of the iron and steel industry, as G.W.F. Hallgarten assumes,[3] whether it was the teachings of the neo-mercan-tilists, with their view of Great Power relations as a struggle over mar-kets and resources; or the ideas of the neo-Rankeans, with their con-ception of the three world empires (the British Empire, the USA and Russia) determining the future of the world and compelling Germany to choose between decline to the status of an exclusively European iden-tity or lifting herself to the rank of a fourth world empire ('World Power or Decline'); or whether it was Mahan's teaching that only sea-power guaranteed global significance (an idea which clearly fascinated Wilhelm II and which Tirpitz utilised to push through the construction of a battleship fleet designed for a decision in the North Sea) — one thing is certain: of essential importance was the Kaiser's decision to seek for the Reich no less than 'parity of status' (*Gleichberechtigung*) with Britain, if not to usurp Britain's position as a German inheritance. At least this is how Bethmann Hollweg described the Kaiser's inten-tions in 1903:

> His basic and primary idea is to destroy England's position in the world to the advantage of Germany; therefore — it is the Kaiser's firm conviction — we need a navy and, to build it, a great deal of money; since only a wealthy country can provide it, Germany shall become wealthy; hence the encouragement given to industry and the

anger of the farmers, who protest against this policy to save themselves from ruin . . . [4]

To the agrarians it was and remained 'that hideous fleet', which they
were persuaded to accept only through the concession of high agrarian
duties.[5] The fleet was to be completed by 1918-20, with sixty capital
ships against ninety British ships, to be employed as a diplomatic lever
and, if it should come to that, as a military weapon against Britain.

At the same time Germany actively applied her so-called *Weltpolitik*
in all parts of the globe, thereby creating frictions and antagonism,
striving for spheres of influence in China, Turkey and South America,
and above all seeking additional colonies in Africa and the South Seas.
If one looks at economic rivalries, one notices that during the 1890s
these existed principally with the protectionist powers, with the USA
and Russia. The anti-English turn in German policy is not explicable in
economic terms alone. Since this did have economic motivation, it was
fear that Britain or the Empire might soon go over to protectionism,
with the result that key markets would then be lost to the German
export industry. For the rest, Great Britain seemed to be blocking
German colonial expansion, even in its attempts to acquire the possessions of older or smaller colonial powers. (See the negotiations with
London on the 'partition' of the Portuguese colonies after 1898 and
again in 1913-14, or over the partition of the Belgian Congo in 1913-
14). German public opinion, at least great parts of the politically and
economically leading groups — looking at the vast colonial acquisitions
of the other Great Powers — believed themselves entitled to such acquisitions also; they spoke (e.g. Hans Delbrück, Friedrich Naumann,
Max Weber, the so-called liberal imperialists) about a coming redistri-
bution of the globe — in one form or another. In fact, even after 1912,
almost nothing was achieved in this direction. Ultimately this weakened
the position of the so-called Anglophiles in Germany, intensified the
impatience of German public opinion and provoked strong criticism of
the Government.

Nevertheless a clear continuity of aims is discernible. Those colonies,
and the 'conglomerate aim' of a *German Central Africa* (a kind of
'German India'), on which Chancellor Bethmann Hollweg had set his
hopes in 1912, reappeared after the outbreak of war (and as early as
August 1914) in the official list of acquisitions to accrue to Germany in
consequence of a German victory, a list drawn up by Colonial Secretary
Solf at the request of Chancellor Bethmann Hollweg. The coveted pos-

sessions included all of Angola, the northern half of Mozambique, the Belgian Congo and French Equatorial Africa as far as Lake Chad (in 1911 Kiderlen-Wachter had demanded the whole of the French Congo), a part of Senegal as far as Timbuctoo, with the Niger forming the northern boundary. The most important were the copper mines of Katanga and the railway line linking it to Benguela, which Germany had aspired to well before 1914. At this stage it was still uncertain whether Britain would wage war *à outrance*. Should she do so and be defeated, then the riches of Nigeria (among other territories) were to be forfeited to Germany as a rounding-off of the territories already listed. As late as the autumn of 1916, during the preparations of Bethmann Hollweg's 'peace offer', and at his behest, the Imperial Naval Office and the Admiralty advanced demands for naval bases in Dacar, in the Azores, on the Cape Verde Islands in order to secure German maritime lines of communications with South America, Africa and the Pacific.

From the autumn of 1914 on, all these overseas aims became purely academic, for Germany was cut off from the world and entangled in a war which made her a beleaguered fortress. How had it come to this? Not least in consequence of *Weltpolitik* and navalism had the Reich become isolated and 'encircled'. Paralleling this situation, the centre of gravity of German policy was transferred back to the Continent, just as armaments priorities were transferred from the fleet back to the army. Here, too, lay the centre of German war aims.

2. Europe – East or West; or: East and West?

If the formation of the Entente Cordiale of 1904 was regarded in Germany as an enormous blow to the power position of the Reich, as numerous contemporaries testify, then the situation became really serious after the Anglo-Russian Agreement of 1907. Naval construction continued at a hectic pace, under Bülow with a series of supplementary estimates and under Bethmann Hollweg with the supplementary bill of 1912. These together represented a challenge which Britain accepted and which, in the end, meant an intolerable financial burden for the Reich. But the German attempt to force the dissolution of the Entente Cordiale in the first Moroccan Crisis; the German ultimatum to Russia to end the Bosnian Crisis; and the German policy during the Second Moroccan Crisis – these three German moves brought home the fact that the army would have the decisive role in a future war. The outcome of the last crisis, known as the Agadir Crisis, was viewed in Germany as a humiliating defeat and was further aggravated by the success of the

Social Democrats in the Reichstag elections of January 1912. This in turn was viewed as a threat to the political and social system and lent credence to the idea — popular in the *élites* — that the only solution lay in war. War simultaneously seemed to secure the stability of the social order and to guarantee the dissolution of the Entente and freedom to pursue an imperialistic policy on a global scale. The collapse of Turkey in October 1912 during the first Balkan war produced the conclusive turning-point in armaments policy in favour of the army (and without any parallel naval increase) in the shape of the great army expansion of 1913. Thus in the budget commission of the Reichstag, in April 1913, the war minister von Heeringen explained, in the presence of Social Democrats, that an enlarged Serbia would tie down Austro-Hungarian forces which would accordingly be absent from the Galician front in a war against Russia; whereas a weakened Turkey, on the other hand, would no longer be in a position to hold down Russian forces in the Caucasus, which thereby became available for use against the Central Powers. Nevertheless he added: 'We cannot compete with the Russian masses; our chance lies in quality.'

Hot on the heels of the mid-November 1912 decision to enlarge the army came the so-called 'War Council' of 8 December 1912. The latest developments had induced the Kaiser to anticipate a degree of *rapprochement* between Germany and Britain. Suddenly all the Kaiser's illusions were dashed by the news of a British warning to Berlin that England could not tolerate any subjugation of France because Britain would then be confronted with a continent under German hegemony. (The Kaiser himself confirmed this anxiety on the part of Britain by his comment on this warning: Haldane had said that 'Britain could not allow Germany to become the leading power on the continent and it (the continent) to be united under Germany's leadership!' — which he called 'unscrupulous, brutish and typically English!') The Kaiser forthwith assembled the military and demanded the immediate opening of hostilities against Britain, France and Russia. Moltke concurred, adding his dictum, 'the sooner the better', since the strength of Germany's land opponents could only continue to grow. But Tirpitz requested a postponement of one and a half years, until the Kiel canal had been deepened for capital ships and the U-boat base on Heligoland had been completed. The 'not before' of the navy and the 'no later than' deadline of the army led to the appointment of a date, of an optimal moment, for the war now held to be inevitable.

The fact that neither the Chancellor nor the Foreign Secretary was present at this conference in no way diminishes its significance, for both were immediately informed of its result and subsequently acted in complete conformity with the procedures agreed upon. What followed was the army build-up already referred to (and described by Gerhard Ritter as Bethmann Hollweg's greatest act of statesmanship) and the deepening of the Kiel canal which was completed 23 June 1914 with the effect that the fleet could be transferred between the North Sea and the Baltic Sea. (In the meantime, on 1 April 1913, the General Staff lapsed the Great Mobilisation Plan East, thus establishing the onslaught on France as the first German act of war, regardless of where and under which circumstances the war might begin. Moltke further sharpened the Schlieffen Plan by incorporating Ludendorff's plan for a *coup de main* against the Belgian fortress at Liége immediately after the proclamation of mobilisation.) As agreed upon on 8 December 1912 the people were psychologically prepared for the great war against Russia by a press campaign under the slogan of the coming 'struggle of races' between Teutons and Slavs, a slogan which was used not only by the Kaiser and Moltke, but even by the Chancellor (although in an indirect form) in his 7 April 1913 speech in the Reichstag on the army bill. In doing so he tried to win the votes of the Russophobe Social Democrats and at the same time to provoke Russia which had to be manoeuvred into the position of the attacker. At the same time Bethmann Hollweg worked to restrain Austria from prematurely drawing her sword and to secure the neutrality of England.

The net effect of developments generally in the year 1913 merely served to aggravate the situation in which Moltke found himself. The French replied with the three-year-service period (which Wilhelm II called 'a provocation'), the Russians in the autumn of 1913 with the Suchomlinov Plan, which would have produced in 1916-17 an enormous numerical and technical upgrading of the Russian army. Indeed by virtue of these very reforms, in Moltke's judgement, neither of these Powers was ready for war in 1914. Accordingly on 20 May 1914 he urged the Foreign Secretary von Jägow to 'attune our policy to an early initiation of war'. Jägow was reluctant to bring it on, but equally reluctant to avoid it, should the opportunity arise. He commented: 'If war appears inevitable, then one should not leave it to the enemy to dictate the moment, but choose it for oneself.' Sarajevo presented this opportunity and had also the advantage of guaranteeing the collaboration of Austria-Hungary. Both Austria-Hungary and Turkey were showing signs of coming to terms with the West, or at least with Russia, and as time wore on the internal coherence of the Austrian army was increasingly jeopardised.

Also very precarious at this time was the economic and financial situation of the Reich and its economy, already feeling the squeeze of its chronic capital shortage, at that moment particularly in the Balkan states and in Turkey in competititon with France, England and Russia. Meanwhile German public opinion was demanding with ever-increasing vigour that the idea of a Berlin-Constantinople-Baghdad Axis be made a firm reality and not just a slogan. On the other hand, France had been throwing stones in the path of Germany's peaceful infiltration (*penetration pacifique*) since 1911, especially regarding the acquisition of ore mines and prospective rights in the frontier ore regions of Longwy, Briey and Nancy. This was annoying for German heavy industry which possessed coal but not iron. A deputation of German industrialists spoke to the former Italian minister of commerce Nitti, 'openly of the need to lay their hands on the iron basis of French Lorraine; war seemed to them a matter for industry'.

The feeling of being the object of French hostility was very wide-spread in German economic and military circles. In November 1913 the Belgian ambassador, Baron Beyens, reported to his minister his famous conversation with Moltke wherein Moltke had predicted that 'war with France was near, nearer than you think'. Baron Beyens went on to report what he called 'the real reasons for (Moltke's) militant attitude':

The generals like many of their compatriots are tired of watching France stand up to Germany on the most difficult political issues, of constantly setting itself up against Germany, of involving it in failures, of objecting to Germany's hegemony or to the fact that the German Empire exercises a predominant influence in Europe and of resisting Germany's colonial wishes; they are tired of watching France constantly increase its army in desperation so as to maintain the balance of power which they believe has in fact long ceased to exist.[6]

Two months later, in January 1914, the Chancellor Bethmann Hollweg repeated such ideas in a conversation with the French ambassador Jules Cambon, where he complained about French obstruction to Germany's policy in Turkey:

Germany sees every day the rapid growth of her population, her merchant fleet, her trade and her industry. Even if you were to deny her that which is the legitimate need of every living and growing organism, you would not be able to arrest her development; but you French will then ensure that you will find yourselves in conflict with us not only in Asia Minor but everywhere.[7]

The Chancellor's range for decision-making was limited. Under the constitutional make-up of the German Empire it was quite difficult to ignore the judgement of military experts in deference to higher political considerations. If the Chancellor sought to pursue 'a policy of diagonals', political realities dictated that his policy could be diametrically (Hildebrand)[8] opposed to that of the military; for the final decision must necessarily favour those with the greater political weight – the Crown, the military, the parties of the right, agrarians and industry, and the bulk of public opinion which was set against France, against Russia and even against Britain and had geared itself to the liberating war. The author of the work *World Policy Without War* stated in 1913 that a sentiment was growing which already represented almost the entire German public opinion which declared: 'We can only win the freedom of our activities in world politics through a Great European War.'

Moreover, Chancellor Bethmann Hollweg (who was one of the largest landowners of Prussia, if not exactly descended from the oldest aristocracy, yet a conservative official of Wilhelm II) was neither enigmatic nor a colourless figure without personal attributes. In domestic politics he approved neither democracy nor parliamentarianism – both completely unthinkable for a man in his position – but he differed from heavy industry and the military in that he recognised that a great war could not be waged without the willing acquiescence of the Social Democrats, and in his foreign policy he kept this thought in the forefront of his thinking. He was a Russophobe like Moltke (1912, 1914), sharing his wish permanently to weaken Russia. Against France he emphatically supported the claim of the rapidly growing German population to a 'place in the sun' (as in January 1914 with Cambon, when he protested against French competition in Turkey). He believed too that the growing might of Germany and the growing risk of war must compel Britain to relinquish the principle of the Balance of Power and to recognise Germany's leadership role on the continent of Europe, an idea he shared with Wilhelm II. Was this really a policy of *detente* or rather a forward policy of expansive demands? But this itself, the growing might and power of Germany, appeared to be at risk, in the spring of 1914, for beyond 1916-17 the necessary pre-conditions for a victory in the military sense could no longer be guaranteed. It may be a matter for some discussion as to whether a war conceived of in such terms can be called a 'preventive war', in which context we should not overlook the fact that at that time war was still regarded as a legitimate instrument of politics. As Zara S. Steiner of Cambridge University says: 'When war was considered, it was not thought of in modern terms. Except for a few sensitive observers, military action in the old style was a possible extension of diplomacy.'[9]

In the crisis of July 1914, Berlin did manage to press Russia into the role of aggressor, as Admiral von Müller wrote in his diary on August 1st: 'The mood is brilliant. The government has managed magnificently to make us appear the attacked party.' This was necessary to get the support of German Social Democrats and by this the thesis of the 'surprise attack' could be constructed. And this thesis provided the genesis of the war aims in the demands for guarantees and securities against a new 'surprise attack' by three Great Powers on the Reich. But Berlin failed to secure the neutrality of Britain, even for the first weeks of the war. This had been much desired by the military, who further believed that if England did participate, her military involvement on the Continent would not be à outrance. They expected the British army would rather limit itself to defence of its harbour bases and were astonished in finding it on the left wing of the French army. Moltke had spoken to Jagow in a completely contemptuous manner in respect of the 150,000 British troops; and the Kaiser prayed to God in August 1914 that the British would cross the path of the German army so that they could be thrashed. The same hope is confirmed in the diary of General von Wenninger, military envoy of the Bavarian King.

Here we encounter the faith in German invincibility, derived from the army, but fostered even in the schools and churches, and posited on three assumptions: (1) the higher art of war (Schlieffen pontificated that the 'key to victory' was safely in the hands of the General Staff); (2) better training and, in addition, better equipment, in 1914 at any rate; (3) higher morale. Thus it would be possible to triumph against difficult odds by taking the offensive.

3. The First World War: Imperial Germany Expecting Victory

German historians often emphasise that Germany wanted nothing else but to break up the 'encirclement' by the Entente. What would this mean for France? France was the opponent which was to be defeated first, and indeed for a few days in late August/early September 1914 France appeared to have been beaten. France as well as Belgium and Holland are referred to in Chancellor Bethmann Hollweg's much-quoted 'September Programme'. It is a programme of diagonals or compromises. It seeks to avoid annexations in the grand manner, as was demanded by an ecstatic public opinion and in numerous sub-missions during the first flush of victory; annexations were to be con-fined to what was considered militarily indispensable or vitally impor-tant to industry. Instead, power was to be clothed in a more modern form through the *Mitteleuropa* programme. It was first submitted to the Chancellor by Walther Rathenau in 1912 and was now brought to his attention once more. It was to be a customs and economic associa-tion embracing France, Belgium, Holland, Denmark, Austria-Hungary, Poland (!) and possibly Italy, Sweden and Norway as well, 'with apparent parity of status among members but in fact under German management'. (This was the goal of the big banks and of the modern export-orientated industries, especially of the electrical and chemical branches, which had first of all to carry the day on the domestic political front against the exponents of protectionism, agrarians and heavy industry).

Still, France was to be reduced to a second rank power. The opening paragraph of the September Programme reads: 'The general aim of war':

Security for the German Reich in west and east for all imaginable time. For this purpose France must be so weakened as to make her revival as a great power impossible for all time. Russia must be thrust back as far as possible from Germany's eastern frontier and her domination over the non-Russian vassal peoples broken.

France was to be disarmed, her fortresses demolished, deprived of most of her colonies, rendered financially dependent, economically retarded by the cession of Longwy-Briey, and compelled to renounce her alliances with Russia and Britain. This situation would have been scarcely veiled by the offensive-defensive alliance with the Reich. Her bondage would have been alleviated at best by Germany's self-interest in settled commercial and economic relations, by France's acceptance as an integral part in the planned European customs union. Britain was to be excluded from the French market, at least, as Rathenau expected, until she would join this union, whose defensive function could then be applied against the USA.

Directed against France and still more against Britain was the aim of converting Belgium into a 'vassal state'. She should be joined closely to Germany, militarily, politically and economically, after she had lost the gateway-fortress of Liége, perhaps also the port of Antwerp, and possibly been extended by the accession of the French Channel ports of Calais, Boulogne and Dunkirk, thus affording the German Reich direct access to the Atlantic. The aim of mastering Belgium was adhered to until the end of the war, even if the form of mastery was envisaged, varying with the war situation, in increasingly direct form; in which context Chancellor Bethmann Hollweg several times mentioned Belgium *and* Poland as the two East-West invasion points of the enemy to be brought under German control. Luxembourg, then associated with Germany in customs and railway agreements, was to become a member-state of the German Reich. Even Holland, together with its rich colonies including present-day Indonesia, was to be brought closer to Germany, albeit in a carefully indirect way.

The campaign in France was to have run its course in about 6-8 weeks, with Troyes, half-way between Paris and Verdun, as the point where the French armies were to be enveloped according to the Schlieffen Plan, or to a somewhat modified plan. The subsequent campaign against Russia was planned as a pincer movement of the Germans from the north and the Austrians from the south. For six weeks, until the main force of the German army had effected the destruction of the French army and had been transferred for action in the East, the Russian assault was to be held in check by the Austro-Hungarian army in Galicia and by a small German force of six corps in East Prussia. Enthralled by the 'short war illusion', the German planners did not calculate on a Napoleonic march to Moscow, but rather on rapid defeat of the Russian field army, at least to the point where an isolated Tsardom, fighting alone on the Continent after the elimination of France, could be brought to the peace table. The General Staffs and Foreign Offices in Vienna and Berlin hoped for labour unrest in St Petersburg and the industrial centres and worked towards rebellious movements in Finland, the Ukraine and Poland (here particularly on the part of Zionists). This would hamper Russian military operations while simultaneously facilitating the 'severance' of the western non-Russian nationalities from the Tsarist empire. Russia should be weakened also economically by means of an imposed and onerous commercial treaty — Russia opened to German industrial products and German grain,

Germany to be closed to Russian grain imports — and diplomatically by the forfeiture of its alliances with France and Britain.

The result of both campaigns — both of them to be implemented in 1914, together with the crushing and occupation of Serbia — would have been a kind of Continental alliance pointed against Britain, or at least the 'neutralisation' of Russia. But how would Britain react? Driven out of France, cut off from Russia by Turkey and in the Baltic, Britain would have had no option but either to recognise Germany's *fait accompli* or to wage a naval war in anticipation of an American alliance.

The first alternative may have been preferred by the 'Anglophile' Bethmann Hollweg. His aim was, as he said, the creation of a 'West European cultural block' against the Muscovite Empire. It was for this reason, during the first months of the war, and with the acquiescence of Tirpitz, that he successfully opposed the immediate employment of the fleet, in order to preserve it as an intact lever for diplomatic use against Great Britain. But the question is, after all, whether the German 'nation', or its politically and economically anti-Western orientated social elites (profoundly anti-English in temperament since August 1914 at the latest, since the 'racial treason' of the Anglo-Saxons), was willing to forego a military victory over Britain. To Erzberger, for instance, who was a leading spokesman of the centre and a man well-connected with heavy industry, this was quite unthinkable in October 1914. Britain, too, must be brought to her knees. If this was not possible in the current war, for reasons of German naval unpreparedness, then certainly in a future war. During the years 1916 and 1917, after it had become clear how difficult it was to bring down Britain militarily, the Kaiser quite openly spoke of a 'second Punic war'.

4. After the Battle of the Marne — November 1914 to November 1918

After the miscarriage of the original German war plan — in the first thrust on the Marne in September, again in the second thrust in Flanders in November 1914 — everything had a different countenance, at least for those very few in Germany who had grasped the true import of the recent fighting. This was equally true in the case of the Austrians, who had suffered an even more crushing defeat in Galicia. But the war which was expected to last no longer than 3-4 months went on as a war of strategic stopgap measures for another four years, albeit in a form totally at variance with German plans and expectations. What then became of Germany's war aims?

After the battles of Langemarck and Ypres, Falkenhayn, as Moltke's successor, described the German army as a 'broken tool' and demanded of the political leadership a separate peace with Russia (an idea acquired from the anti-British Tirpitz) so that, thus relieved, he might at least salvage for Germany a victory over France and even England. When Bethmann Hollweg embarked on his highly secretive endeavours to bring Russia to a separate peace, he did so in full awareness of the three Allies' London Agreement of 5 September 1914, after which a separate peace with Germany could not be concluded without leading directly to negotiations for a general peace. And this would have meant, for Germany, complete renunciation of her war aims. (Indeed, Germany was already having to water them down in respect of Russia.) But Bethmann Hollweg knew that this would never have the approval of German public opinion, which he had by his own decision left in the dark as to the true outcome of the battle of the Marne, and which was misled as to the true significance of the victory of Tannenberg. So his hands were tied. In any event, Russia was still the main enemy for the Austro-Hungarian and Turkish allies. (He was also aware that the Tsar and the Russian Government would be amenable to a separate peace, if at all, only in the event of total defeat.) Thus he continued the energetic prosecution of the war against Russia in 1915, and against Serbia as well. Then came the occupation of Poland and splendid successes were registered in the east. Now as always whenever the war was going well against Russia, the political leaders and particularly the Foreign Office (Jagow) manifested a revival of interest in the original plan to permanently weaken Russia, to banish the Russian nightmare, by detaching the western territories from the eastern colossus. In 1915, 1916 and 1917 the Chancellor even announced publicly in the Reichstag — not least with an eye to President Wilson and liberal circles in the West — that the German aim was the 'liberation' of the non-Russian nationalities from the yoke of Tsarism. A comprehensive programme for the encouragement of revolution was intended to further this end, as was also the case with the creation of the Kingdom of Poland in November 1916. (To be sure, this remained a bone of contention between the Central Powers in their haggling over a Prussian-Polish or an Austro-Polish solution.)

However, to smooth the path of the separate peace-feelers towards Russia, the German Chancellor had long before pointed the spearhead of his foreign policy against Britain. So he crested the wave of popular hatred of Britain, even artificially stimulating it in the interest of raising morale. In December 1914, in his second Reichstag speech of the war,

he still blamed Russia for causing the war in the technical sense (as he
had in his speech of 4 August), but now he emphatically burdened
Britain with the essential responsibility for the war as the generator and
motive force behind the 'policy of encirclement'. In this speech he proclaimed that it had been the aim of his policy even before the war to
press England, through the weight of German power, into abandoning
the principle of the balance of power, and that this principle would
now, as a result of the war, be laid aside for all time as far as the new
Europe was concerned. Or as he shortly beforehand vouchsafed to a
high-ranking military officer, who was to pass it on to the leaders of the
'patriotic' parties:

> The aim of this war . . . is not the restoration of the European
> balance of power but on the contrary the permanent elimination of
> what has hitherto been described as the European balance of power
> and the establishment of German hegemony in Europe.[10]

Or again in his speech of 19 August 1915, where he called for perse-
verance in the defensive struggle 'until we have fought and won all
possible material [*reale*] guarantees and securities, so that none of our
enemies, either singly or in concert, will ever again dare take arms
against us'. (This was the defensive garb for the formulation of German
war aims as coined by him in August/September 1914 with President
Wilson in mind.) Whatever the tactical and psychological implications in
the diagonal policy between Social Democracy (positively orientated
towards a war of defence) and the bourgeois parties (far superior in
terms of domestic political influence and determined to enlarge German
power), the effect was that any thought of a retreat to the *status quo
ante* – as far as Germany was concerned – was blocked thereby.

The 'war aims majority' of the Reichstag parties and the 'war aims
movement' of the leading economic interest groups and intellectual
luminaries opposed all suggestion of a peace of renunciation. The
Government could not completely neglect these groups, particularly
since industry was so closely meshed with the parties (especially with
the Free-Conservatives, the National-Liberals and the Centre Party),
with the high administration in Prussia and the Reich and – not least –
with the army and the navy. The demands of the six largest economic
interest groups of industry, agriculture and commerce cannot be lightly
dismissed as 'reveries of German patriots', after the manner of Gerhard
Ritter. They found support among the overwhelming bulk of the intelli-

gentsia; the ratio of the signatories of the so-called professorial sub-
mission to that of moderates was about 10: 1 (in 1915 as well as in
1917). All of them demanded, along with *Mittelafrika* and *Mitteleuropa*
and commercial guarantees, land acquisitions (in the form of annexations) and buffer states to east and west. Regarding annexations in the
east (the Polish border strip and Courland), the idea, already virulent in
the movement for internal colonisation in the pre-war period, was
ventilated in order that the rural-farming element as opposed to the
urban-industrial complex might be re-inforced through the propagation
of settlement by German peasant farmers including the German
colonists hitherto resident within Russia – thus avoiding a partition of
the big East Elbian estates. Both directions, west and east, will now be
briefly referred to once again.

First a few remarks on the 'western' orientation, whose principal
advocate was industry. Indeed in 1917 the spokesmen of heavy industry
informed Reich Chancellor Michaelis that they would be willing to
fight on for another ten years for the sake of Longwy-Briey alone. Yet
it is unquestionably the case that the power-political factor also came
into consideration, as when the Krupp memorandum said: 'A France
without appreciable ore and coal supplies can no longer be a menace
economically in the world market or politically in the council of the
Great Powers.'[11] The power-political factor was even more significant
for those who viewed Britain as the real foe and in the expectations
which were associated with a military pre-eminence over Belgium and
possibly, too, over the northern coast of France. Krupp believed, as
did Tirpitz, that Britain would be forced into friendship by means of a
German presence on the Channel: ' . . . there we would be at the spinal
cord of British world supremacy, a position – perhaps the only one –
which could give us the lasting friendship of Britain.'[12] This expectation was completely contradicted by all historical experience. Whatever
the purely strategic considerations of that moment had been, it is unquestionably true that Falkenhayn's attack on Verdun in 1916 (which
failed), like the decision for unrestricted U-boat warfare (which did not,
as Admiral Capelle promised, force Britain to make peace within five
months, but instead brought America into the war), belongs to the
pattern of thought of those favouring the western orientation, the
opponents of Britain, in other words.

As far as the so-called 'Eastern' orientation is concerned, its alternatives can best be elucidated by reference to the contrasting views of
the two professors of East European history at the University of Berlin,

Otto Hoetzsch and Theodor Schiemann. Hoetzsch, a conservative, yet a moderate by reputation, held the view that the gigantic state of Russia could never be completely conquered, that it deserved to be maintained as a conglomerate state (*Gesamtstaat*) with centuries of development behind it, to be spared and won over to friendship — but after the victory over France and over the Russian field-armies. That did not prevent him advocating the severance of the Polish border strip or annexations in the north-east, though only as far as Riga because the further Baltic coast to Reval could never be maintained indefinitely against Russian pressure. For the rest, Hoetzsch regarded Britain as Germany's principal opponent which had to be beaten if there was to be an assured future for German world standing and commerce. (In this respect he was on common ground with Tirpitz, Krupp and company.) It was therefore necessary to control Belgium, particularly the port of Antwerp and if possible the Channel ports as well. Pan-Slavism was to be eradicated by means of the closest possible association of the Reich with Austria-Hungary, which indeed was on no account to be permitted to acquire the future Polish state, for such a union would make it a Slavic state and as such useless for Germany; further by joint mastery over the Balkans and joint penetration of Turkey.

Completely contrary were the views of Schiemann, a German Balt and a mortal foe of Russia, which he viewed as a hodge-podge of peoples that must be broken up by the severance of its non-Russian nationalities so that the menacing colossus might be weakened once and for all. Since 1848 such ideas had been common currency among German liberals, Democrats and Social Democrats — even Karl Marx had once urged a European War of liberation against Tsarism — and among Catholics, too, for Catholic Poland (as Catholic Lithuania) and the Vatican were esteemed in Vienna and Berlin as potential moral allies. For Chancellor Bethmann Hollweg these ideas represented an ideological legacy from his family, inherited through his grandfather. The elder Bethmann Hollweg was the founder and leader of the Prussian *Wochemblattpartei* which, during the Crimean War wanted to bring Prussia onto the side of the Western Powers, France and Britain, against Russia. (This was prevented by Bismarck.) At that time it was the elder Bethmann Hollweg who developed the idea that it was possible permanently to weaken Russia only by revolutionising the non-Russian nationalities and detaching them from the Russian Empire.

This train of thought culminated in the Peace of Brest-Litovsk which severed from Russia a whole chain of buffer states — Finland, the

Baltic provinces (to become a part of Germany or at least closely attached to the Reich), Poland (with an Austro-Hungarian Archduke on its throne but bound to the German Reich by close political, military and economic ties), the Ukraine, the Crimea, the Caucasian states, particularly Georgia.

But it would be quite misleading to deduce the principles which inspired this peace solely or primarily from the realm of ideas. Apart from frontier security, alliance considerations and power politics (the rolling back of Russia), economic interests were also at stake. In this sense the treaties of Brest-Litovsk, like the simultaneous peace of Bucharest with Rumania, were genuine instances of imperialism, regarded here as a policy determined primarily or substantially by economic factors. Ukrainian grain supplies for starving Austria may be viewed as an expedient of war economics, but not so with the iron ore of Krivoi Rog in the Ukraine, the manganese of Tschiaturi in Georgia or the petroleum of the Caucasus and Rumania. These were long-term economic objectives to meet the raw-material requirements of German industry; they by no means came into view for the very first time — though certainly gained in importance thereby — when the decisions of the 1916 Allied world economic conference in Paris threatened to victimise Germany and exclude it from the raw materials and markets of the world. During the war itself, grand designs were already in hand for the opening up of the occupied eastern territories by means of joint stock companies and study projects specially established for this purpose (above all in areas like railway and port construction and mining). How firmly these annexations and satellite states were believed to be in Germany's grasp may be seen from the fact that in October 1918 the German Government regarded itself as being in a position to demand of President Wilson (under the containment of Bolshevism slogan) that he acknowledge the *status quo* attained in the East.

At least partly because of the immoderate German demands, peace was concluded only belatedly in the East. It was approved by all the bourgeois parties in the Reichstag, and rejected only by the Independent Social Democrats, while the Majority Social Democrats abstained from voting. Thereafter there remained the determination to see the war through to a victorious conclusion in the West as well, and, so it was hoped, before the Americans could enter the fray in any meaningful sense. It cannot be assumed that in the event of victory in the West German war aims there would have diverged markedly from those drawn up by the Reich Government in September 1914. If at that time these aims were justified by reference to the great sacrifices already made, this motive must have weighed all the more heavily after four years of warfare. Astonishingly enough, the political and military leaders even in 1918 were still holding a series of war aims conferences, when the chances of ever realising such aims were dwindling steadily.

If in 1918, in consequence of the eastern policy of Ludendorff and Kuhlmann/Hintze, the pivot of interest appeared to have undergone a notable shift towards the East, still it must not be lost sight of that the Balkans, Turkey and even the Austrian-Hungarian ally themselves became (what I venture to call) a German war aim, and this by means of negotiations — continued right up to the last month of the war — for the closest possible political, economic and military association of the two empires. (In a reversal of 1866, the intention was to restore some form of the German Confederation, but this time under Hohenzollern leadership — yet with scrupulous regard for the prestige of the more venerable Habsburgs) For at the centre of political and economic objectives there remained the *Mitteleuropa* idea, but it is in the form of a completely free trade zone or, in deference to the protectionist lobby (Prussian and Hungarian agrarians and heavy industry) as a system of graduated tariffs. There remained too, the prospect of a world which might resemble the picture drawn in 1916 by von Falkenhausen (a high-ranking official in the Prussian Ministry for Agriculture):

> To match the great, closed economic bodies of the United States, the British and the Russian Empires with an equally solid economic block representing all European states, or at least those of central Europe, under German leadership, with the twofold purpose: 1. of assuring the members of this whole, and particularly Germany, the mastery of European market, and 2. of being able to lead the entire economic strength of allied Europe into the field as a unified force, in the struggle with those world powers over the conditions of the admission of each to the markets of the others. [Schoeneback, another high ranking official and advocate of the customs union idea, added to those three closed economic bodies a fourth: 'Japan with China.'] [13]

As justification and an aim of war, Bethmann Hollweg's private secretary, Kurt Riezler, offered the following view in a diary entry of 1 August 1916:

. . . the threefold sense of the war is: defence against present-day France, preventive war against the Russia of the future (as such, too late), struggle with Britain for world supremacy.[14]

This was written down before America entered the war which completely changed the situation of all belligerents and all of Europe.

Notes

1. Ludwig Dehio, *Deutschland und die Weltpolitik im 20. Jahrhundert* (Munich, 1955), translated as *Germany and World Politics* (London and New York, 1959).
2. Hans Ulrich Wehler (ed.), *Imperialismus* (Cologne/Berlin, 1970); Volker R. Berghahn, *Der Tirpitz-Plan, Genesis und Verfall einer innenpolitischen Krisenstrategie unter Wilhelm II* (Dusseldorf, 1971), and *Germany and the Approach of War in 1914* (London, 1973).
3. G.W.F. Hallgarten, *Imperialismus vor 1914,* 2nd ed., 2 vols. (Munich, 1963).
4. Bethmann Hollweg, 1903, in *Das Tagebuch der Baronin Spitzemberg,* ed. by R. Vierhaus (Gottingen, 1960), p. 428.
5. Eckart Kehr, *Schlactflottenbau und Parteipolitik* (Berlin, 1930).
6. F. Fischer, *Krieg der Illusionen: Die deutsche Politik von 1911 bis 1914* (Dusseldorf, 1969), translated as *War of Illusions: German Policies from 1911 to 1914* (London/New York, 1975), p. 228.
7. *Ibid.,* pp. 444-5.
8. Gerhard Hildebrand, *Sozialistiche Auslandspolitik* (Jena, 1912).
9. Zara S. Steiner, *The Foreign Office and Foreign Policy, 1898-1914* (Cambridge, 1969), p. 212.
10. Fischer, *War of Illusions,* p. 547.
11. F. Fischer, *Griff nach der Weltmacht: Die Kriegszielpolitik des Kaiserlichen Deutschland, 1914-1918* (Dusseldorf, 1961), translated as *Germany's Aims in the First World War* (London/New York, 1967), p. 170.
12. *Ibid.*
13. Fischer, *War of Illusions,* p. 539.
14. *Ibid.,* p. 549.

CONTRIBUTORS

Robert Craig Brown, was born in Rochester, New York and educated at the University of Rochester and the University of Toronto. After teaching at the University of Calgary he joined the Department of History at the University of Toronto where he is currently Professor of History and Associate Chairman. A former editor of the *Canadian Historical Review,* he is co-editor of *Confederation to 1949* (Scarborough, 1966) and *The Canadians, 1867-1967* (Toronto, 1968), co-author of *Canada Views the United States* (Seattle, 1967) and of *Canada, 1896-1921: A Nation Transformed* (Toronto, 1974), and author of *Canada's National Policy, 1883-1900* (Princeton, 1964) and *Robert Laird Borden, A Biography, Volume I, 1854-1914* (Toronto, 1975).

Edward M. Coffman, a Kentuckian, is Professor of History at the University of Wisconsin, Madison. Prior to coming to Madison in 1961, he served two years as an infantry officer, taught at Memphis State University, and was a Research Associate with the George C. Marshall Research Foundation. In 1969-70, he was the Visiting Dwight D. Eisenhower Professor at Kansas State University. His publications include *The Hilt of the Sword: The Career of Peyton C. March* (Wisconsin, 1966) and *The War To End All Wars: The American Military Experience in World War I* (New York, 1968). A former Guggenheim Fellow, he has also served on the Advisory Committee of the Department of the Army Historical Program and the National Historical Publications and Records Commission. Currently, he is working on a social history of the American peacetime Army, 1784-1940.

Fritz Fischer, a native of Bavaria, Germany, was educated at the Universities of Erlangen and Berlin. From 1935 he taught Church History at the University of Berlin where, in 1937, he received his PhD (Dr phil). Following his war-time military service, in 1948 he was appointed to the Chair of Medieval and Modern History at the University of Hamburg where since 1973 he has been Professor Emeritus. In addition to several books and articles on German intellectual history, he has published *Griff nach der Weltmach: Die Kriegszielpolitik des kaiserlichen Deutschland, 1914-1918* (Dusseldorf, 1961), translated into French, Italian and Japanese eds., in English as *Germany's Aims in the First World War* (London/New York, 1967); and *Krieg der Illusionen: Die deutsche Politik von 1911 bis 1914* (Dusseldorf, 1969), translated as *War of Illusions: German Policies from 1911 to 1914* (London/New York, 1975), two books which caused much world-wide discussion. He has lectured widely at universities in Europe, the United States, Canada and Japan. In 1964-5 he was made a member of the Institute for Advanced Study at Princeton University. In 1969-70 he was a Visiting Professor at Oxford University. In 1971, he was elected Corresponding Member of the British Academy. He is now working on the problem of continuity in German history after World War I.

John Gooch, was born in England and educated at King's College, University of London. A lecturer in History at the University of Lancaster since 1969, he has also been Visiting Lecturer in Modern History at the University of Liverpool, 1974-75. He is the author of *The Plans of War: The General Staff and British Military Strategy, 1900-1916* (London, 1974), and of a number of articles on British military affairs. A Fellow of the Royal Historical Society, he currently holds a British Academy Solfson Fellowship at Rome.

Barry Hunt was educated at the Royal Military College of Canada, the University of Western Ontario and Queen's University. From 1956-67 he served as a regular officer in The Royal Canadian Regiment. Since 1967 he has lectured in Imperial and Naval History at the R.M.C. In 1974-5 he was Visiting Professor of Military History and Strategic Studies at the University of Western Ontario. He is the author of several articles on British naval history and is now preparing a life of Admiral Sir Herbert Richmond.

Douglas Johnson, Professor of French History at University College, London, since 1968. Formerly Professor of Modern History and Chairman of the School of History at the University of Birmingham, UK. He is the author of *Guizot: Aspects of French History, 1787-1874* (London, 1963); *France and the Dreyfus Affair* (London, 1966); and *A Concise History of France* (London, 1970).

Adrian Preston was educated at the Royal Military College of Canada, University of British Columbia, University of Toronto and University of London, King's College. Since 1965 he has been Associate Professor of History at RMC. In 1971-2 he held the Chair of Military and Strategic Studies at Acadia University, NS. He has published *In*

Relief of Gordon (London, 1967), *The South African Diaries of Sir Garnet Wolseley 1875* (Cape Town, 1971), *The South African Journals of Sir Garnet Wolseley 1879-80* (Cape Town, 1973). He is the co-editor, with Peter Dennis, of *Soldiers as Statesmen* (London, 1976) and *Swords and Covenants: Essays in Honour of the Centenary of the Royal Military College of Canada, 1876-1976* (London, 1976).

John Whittam read History at Worcester College Oxford and then spent two years at St Antony's studying for a B.Phil. and writing a dissertation on Farini. After spending a year as an instructor at the University of Pennsylvania, he lectured at London University, first at Royal Holloway and, between 1962 and 1964, at Westfield College. Since 1964, he has been lecturing at Bristol University. In 1967 he completed his Ph.D. (London University), writing a dissertation on Ricasoli. In 1970-71 he was Alistair Horne Fellow at St Antony's engaged in research on the Risorgimento. He has made several visits to Italy, has published articles on Italian history in the period 1861-1945, and his book on *The Politics of the Italian Army* (London 1977) appeared recently. His teaching commitments include European History since 1815 and a more intensive course on the Fall of France. He is at present engaged on research into Tuscan fascism and the Anglo-Italian war beteen 1940 and 1943.

INDEX